SPEAKING FOR HOWELLS

Charting the Dean's Career through the Language of His Characters

Gregory J. Stratman

University Press of America,® Inc.
Lanham · New York · Oxford

University Press of America,® Inc.
4720 Boston Way
Lanham, Maryland 20706

12 Hid's Copse Rd.
Cumnor Hill, Oxford OX2 9JJ

Printed in the United States of America
British Library Cataloging in Publication Information Available

Library of Congress Cataloging-in-Publication Data

Stratman, Gregory J.
Speaking for Howells : charting the dean's career through the language of his characters / Gregory J. Stratman.
p. cm
Includes bibliographical references (p.) and index.
1. Howells, William Dean, 1837-1920—Characters.
2. Howells, William Dean, 1837-1920—Language.
3. Characters and characteristics in literature.
4. Language and languages in literature.
5. Dialogue in literature. 6. Speech in literature. I. Title.
PS2037.C47 S77 2001 813'.4—dc21 2001027397 CIP

ISBN 0-7618-2013-2 (cloth : alk. paper)
ISBN 0-7618-2014-0 (pbk. : alk. paper)

™ The paper used in this publication meets the minimum requirements of American National Standard for Information Sciences—Permanence of Paper for Printed Library Materials, ANSI Z39.48—1984

Teresa
Wes
Tia
Stacia

To you, my love and thanks.

CONTENTS

PREFACE

This study examines William Dean Howells's intense interest in language, particularly literary language, and it illustrates how his use of language can be studied to indicate the evolution of his career. Since his views on language were so extensive and his canon of works so large, this study focuses on Howells's use of literary dialect in a representative number of works to support the following thesis: Howells's career charted a circular path from romanticism to realism back to romanticism, and the changes that his career experienced can be examined through an analysis of his extensive writings about language and, more specifically, through the language of his literary characters. In the end, this study shows that Howells's comments on language show a man whose opinions were strong and well reasoned but not always consistent and whose own literary works were inconsistent in following his own literary dictates.

ACKNOWLEDGEMENTS

The germ for this study was given to me in 1983 by Gil Youmans, who was then my graduate adviser and my teacher in a seminar entitled The Language of Literature. My seminar paper focused on the usage of literary dialect in the works of several of America's most notable realists. From that relatively immature and superficial study grew a doctoral dissertation that examined the career of William Dean Howells. And from that work, this work has evolved. I owe a great debt of gratitude to Gil Youmans and Don Lance, whose guidance through this study was instrumental.

My gratitude also goes to Elsa Nettels, Professor Emeritus at the College of William and Mary, whose kind response to a letter from a struggling graduate student and her permission to quote from that letter a decade later are both greatly appreciated.

My most heartfelt thanks are reserved for my wife, Teresa, whose patience and confidence have helped me struggle through the various stages of this work. My children – Wes, Tia, and Stacia – have been as supportive and helpful in their individual ways.

INTRODUCTION

Howells in American Literary History

Everybody that reads in America knows about Howells, ...
-- *Anonymous, 1894*

William Dean Howells is an enigmatic figure in American Literature. His contributions to the literature of this country can hardly be overestimated. He opened the field to Western and Southern writers and led the call for a more realistic fiction. He wrote over thirty novels and nearly forty plays. He wrote reviews and editorials on a weekly or monthly basis for over forty years, and his correspondence fills six large volumes.

In 1988, Elsa Nettels published *Language, Race, and Social Class in Howells's America*. That was the first extended study of Howells's commentary on and use of language. Nine years later, she devoted a chapter of her work *Language and Gender in American Fiction* to "The Voices of Men and Women in Howells's Fiction and Drama." Nettels's work will be discussed in the first chapter in positioning it in context with this study.

Howells was not really a man of his times. As with most any literary innovator, he was a man who helped to shape the times. As this study will examine, Howells was a man who charted his own course based on his developing literary conceptions and preferences, and he wanted to bring the whole country on that course with him. Essentially, this study will examine Howells's intense interest in (one could say preoccupation with) language, particularly the language of literature, and it will illustrate how his use of language can be studied to indicate the evolution of his career. Since his views on language were so extensive and his canon of works so large, this study focuses on Howells's use of literary dialect in a representative number of works to support the following thesis: Howells's career charted a circular path from romanticism to realism back again to romanticism, and the changes that his career experienced can be examined through the analysis of his extensive writings about language and, more specifically, the language of his literary characters. In the end, this study will illustrate that Howells's comments on language show a man whose opinions were strong and well reasoned but not always consistent and whose own literary works were inconsistent in following his own literary dictates.

CHAPTER 1

Howells and Language

I explore the common,
I explore and sit at the feet of the familiar, ...
-- *Ralph Waldo Emerson*

In 1837, in his address to the Phi Beta Kappa Society at Harvard University, Ralph Waldo Emerson declared his views on language:

> Life is our dictionary. Years are well spent in country labors; in town; in the insight into trades and manufactures; in frank intercourse with many men and women; in science; in art; to the one end of mastering in all their facts a language by which to illustrate and embody our perceptions. I learn immediately from any speaker how much he has already lived, through the poverty or splendor of his speech. Life lies behind us as the quarry from whence we get tiles and copestones for the masonry of to-day. This is the way to learn grammar. Colleges and books only copy the language which the field and the work-yard made. (98)

That same year, in Martinsville, Ohio, was born the man who would become one of the most influential proponents of Emerson's linguistic dicta -- William Dean Howells.

Howells's reputation is well established in many areas – as novelist, editor, critic, poet, and dramatist. But less recognized are his abilities as a scholar of language. Though never formally trained in the study of language, he developed an expertise that was remarkable. In 1897, Harry Thurston Peck described Howells's ability as a "natural gift of language" (532). And that gift was magnified by Howells's passion for languages. As a boy, he studied five languages simultaneously, learning them on his own despite what he called his "almost entire want of schooling" (*Selected Letters*, v. 1, 375). In an 1892 interview with Franklin Smith, Howells explained:

> I took up Spanish when I was about thirteen or fourteen years old. I studied German at the same time. I got a "little Latin and less Greek" after my day's work was done. I learned to read French from my knowledge of other languages. (quoted in Halfmann, 298)

Later, in the 1860's, while serving as U.S. Consul in Venice, he added Italian to his linguistic repertoire. Eventually, he became sufficiently fluent in Spanish, German, and Italian to translate works from those languages into English. Scattered throughout his writings is evidence not only of his familiarity with foreign idiom (examples of which flowed from his pen fluently and frequently) but of the style and syntax of those languages, as well. For example, in an 1892 letter to Mark Twain, Howells wrote

> What a beautiful book that Prince and Pauper on India paper which you gave Winny is. (There's a High Dutch sentence for you.) (*Twain-Howells*, v. 1, 386)

And in 1909, a letter to Henry James included this comment:

> Incredibly enough we are here, Pilla and I, and the gayer for your heart-friendly letter. (I fall helplessly into the German idiom.) (*Selected Letters*, v. 5, 293)

But as interested as he was in other languages, Howells was most interested in the English language, perhaps more so than in any other topic except literature. His novels, criticism, editorials, and correspondence contain numerous comments (illustrated extensively in Chapter 3) on the English language, ranging from sermons on correct grammar and pronunciation to calls for the use of dialect in literature.

However, this aspect of Howells's abilities and of his work has not been fully explored. Since his role in the development of literary realism is undeniably primary and since his views on language formed a basic tenet of his campaign for realism as the most appropriate method in fiction, his theories of language, specifically literary language, deserve attention, and his accomplishments in the literary usage of language demand recognition.

In a biographical pamphlet on Howells, William Gibson briefly discusses the "Dean's" importance in the history of the language of literature:

> As the vehicle for the "new fiction", Howells advocated, published, and practiced a new, supple colloquial English, taking as his authority writers so diverse as Dante and Emerson, James Russell Lowell and Artemus Ward, Mark Twain and Henry James. The "language of the street" in many regional varieties functions vitally in his own fiction, and he praised it as it appeared in the "local color" stories of Harte, De Forest, Cable, Frederic, Garland, and even Norris and Crane. . . . Mark Twain chiefly created a revolution in the language of fiction; Howells was the architect of the revolution. (39-40)

Gibson stands apart from much of the critical world in claiming Howells's importance in the 19th century's "revolution" in the language of literature, since that aspect of Howells's abilities remains, a century later, largely unrecognized. But Gibson's comments signaled the beginning of the long-overdue realization that Howells played a major role in the evolution of literary American English beginning in the 1870's.

In 1988, sixty-eight years after Howells's death, the first extended study of his interest in language appeared -- *Language, Race, and Social Class in Howells's America* by Elsa Nettels. In the opening lines of the preface, Nettels justifies her work in support of Gibson's claim:

> This study centers on William Dean Howells as a writer about language. To read his fiction, criticism, and letters is to realize that no other American novelist before or since has written so fully about so many aspects of language; no other has commented so often on the habits of speech of characters or placed such importance on speech as an index of their culture and social class. A study of his novels substantiates the statement of William M. Gibson . . . . (ix)

Nettels's work -- a combination of literary criticism and cultural history -- takes a sociolinguistic approach to Howells's fiction, focusing on the social and political implications of language in post-Civil War America. In Howells's heyday, language and its use were the center of much controversy, and Howells was often in the middle of the battles. As much a social critic as a literary one, Howells understood and evoked the power of language in his criticism and fiction. Nettels deliberately "didn't attempt a technical study of dialect but was concerned primarily with questions of characterization and the author's and narrator's attitudes" (Letter from the author, 1988). More specifically, she focuses on the methods Howells used to depict his characters based on their social, racial, and gender differences. Nettels explains that the ability of language to establish social, political, and racial identity was a primary concern in America in the 19th century, and she examines how Howells illustrated that fact in the language of his characters. She later elaborates on this point:

> In rendering the different habits of speech of his characters, Howells dramatized the divisive effects of language, the power of speech to reinforce the barriers that divide the social classes, the races, and the sexes. Indeed, in fiction, if not in life, speech, more powerfully than anything else, creates the reader's impression of a character's culture and distinguishes him or her from persons of a different culture. To study the language of Howells's characters is thus to see the contradiction at the heart of a society that proclaimed itself democratic; it is also to see the contradiction at the heart of Howells's conception of the American realist, whose office was to unite people in recognition of their common humanity, but also faithfully to reveal a society in which language elevates some people above others and so belies the ideal of equality. (5-6)

Nettels's work is neither a technical study nor an evaluative analysis of Howells's use of dialect and vernacular speech; rather, her purpose was "to analyze the effects of dialect and the vernacular in his fiction and to identify the attitudes implicit in his renderings of the speech of his characters" (x). This study differs from Nettels's work in that it focuses on Howells's literary language and dialect from another perspective. The primary focus here will be on Howells's extensive commentary on language, which can be fully understood and adequately examined only by first describing the "linguistic atmosphere" of the American literary scene upon Howells's emergence in the mid-1800's. A close examination of Howells's comments on language helps to piece together his attitudes (one could say his theories) about language, identify the contradictions in these attitudes and theories, reevaluate their importance, and position them within the context of the controversies that existed in the last third of the 19th century.

In light of his theories about language, his works and his development as a writer can be analyzed from a linguistic perspective by studying his use of language in general and of literary dialect in particular. This study surveys the linguistic theories embodied in his critical reviews and editorials. It then charts the evolution of his literary tendencies (or preferences) and analyzes how his literary language reflects that evolution, specifically focusing on the speech of his characters, especially on Basil and Isabel March, a husband and wife patterned loosely after Howells and his own wife. The Marches appear in several of Howells's works throughout his literary career.

This first chapter positions Howells within the literary atmosphere of the 19th century, and Chapter 2 positions him within the linguistic debates that began as soon as the English-speaking immigrants arrived from Great Britain. These debates flourished during the post-Revolution decades and continued through Howells's day. In Chapter 3, Howells's abundant commentary on language -- both literary and non-literary -- is discussed in order to pinpoint his linguistic theory of literary language.

After Howells's linguistic attitudes are presented, his evolution as a writer is examined in light of his views on literary language, with a particular focus on the language of his characters. Chapter 4 evaluates his early works, especially the romanticism of his writing. Chapter 5 charts his path into full-blown realism, examining the changes that are evident in the language of his characters. Chapter 6 examines Howells's approach to realism and dialogue on the stage. The final chapter discusses Howells's return to his romantic tendencies in the waning years of his life and comments on the effects of his attitudes and approach to literary language on the succeeding generations of writers.

While much has been written about Howells as a novelist and critic, and even as a dramatist, little criticism has examined his evolution from romantic to realist to romantic. Even less critical attention has focused on Howells's linguistic commentary. Howells the linguist has been practically untouched.

This study offers this different perspective on Howells. It discusses Howells the linguist and Howells the romantic -- two aspects of Howells largely unexamined, two aspects that would surprise those people whose perception of Howells is based on one overriding impression that has dominated his reputation in the eight decades since his death -- that of a prudish, "smiling aspects" realist. This study will show how Howells's commentary on language and his own literary use of language are important indicators of his literary career. In other words, Howells's attitudes towards language and his use of language illustrate his attitudes towards literature and affect his final literary works.

This study does not attempt a technical dialectal study, nor does it propose to question or belittle Howells's accomplishments in helping to establish realism as the dominant literary movement in the second half of the 19th century. It offers a general examination of the literary dialect of the characters of a man who recognized the power of language to depict reality and to characterize its speakers.

CHAPTER 2

English in America: Seeking Linguistic Independence

> That which distinguishes the literature of one nation from that of another is not so much a difference of thought as of expression.
> *James K. Paulding, 1815*

Many years before the American Revolution, colonial writers recognized the desire and the need to use a language in their writings that would sound native to the ears of their readers. In the early 1700s, the Virginian historian Robert Beverly wrote of the necessity to write "Poetical Stories" and "Romance" in a style and language that differed from those of the Europeans:

> I am an *Indian*, and don't pretend to be exact in my Language. But I hope the Plainness of my Dress, will give him [the reader] the kinder Impressions of my Honesty, which is what I pretend to. Truth . . . depends upon its own intrinsic Value, and, like Beauty, is rather conceal'd, than set off by Ornament. (quoted in Spencer, 9)

Beverly saw the language of European Romance, particularly those from France, as dainty, fluffy, and ornamental. And he knew that such language could neither effectively nor completely express the American experience.

Also in the early 1700s, Cotton Mather, who unreservedly "accepted the necessity of adapting style to milieu" in American writing, understood the practical need of developing a New World-style in order for the writings to be comprehensible to the majority of the reading public. He argued that American writers should express "American Sentiments" in a "Habit and Language" with an "American change." He also resolved in his own writing to touch "everything with an American pen" (quoted in Spencer, 9-10). During the next half-century, few heeded Mather's words, but in 1774, as America fought for political independence, a letter written by a person identified simply as "An American" reiterated Mather's call for another kind of independence:

> The English language has been greatly improved in Britain within a century, but its highest perfection, with every other branch of human knowledge, is perhaps reserved for this Land of light and freedom. As the people through this extensive country will speak English, their advantages for polishing their language will be great and vastly superior to what people in England ever enjoyed. (Mathews, 40)

Though that comment may have been motivated mostly by a revolution-era anti-British sentiment, it did raise an issue that was to become the center of controversy for many decades after the war had ended -- the language of the new nation. That issue was frequently the topic of commentary of America's writers, commentary that was at times vehement, at times conciliatory, at times condescending.

Linguistic freedom seemed to be nearly as important to American writers as political freedom was. They realized that, to sever completely all ties with England, they had to do more than establish an independent government. They had to establish a society and a culture that were both separate and distinct from those of Britain, yet they knew that social and cultural separation was impossible to achieve as long as the vehicle for communication -- the language -- was controlled in England. As James K. Paulding reasoned in 1814, Americans could never be "truly independent till we make our own books, and coin our own words -- two things as necessary to national sovreignty as making laws and coining money" (quoted in Spencer, 57). Paulding's better known contemporary Noah Webster shared that sentiment: ". . . our honor requires us to have a system of our own, in language as well as in government" (quoted in Spencer, 56). Thomas Jefferson approached the issue from a more practical viewpoint in explaining that the "new circumstances under which we are placed call for new words, new phrases, and for the transfer of old words to new objects" (quoted in Spencer, 57). He further contended that the changes that had been occurring and would continue to occur illustrated the richness of the language rather than the debasement of it.

Hugh Blair, one of the most influential critical authorities of the post-revolution era, "encouraged American authors to believe that the utterances of the young nation, unpolished though they were, might surpass in imaginative power the more sophisticated productions of Europe" (quoted in Spencer, 33). The Southern editors Hugh Legare' and J. W. Simmons argued in 1829 that the "very existence of the national mind is contingent on the formation of a 'dialect of our own -- a language as American . . . as the principles and opinions which it shall embody'" (quoted in Spencer, 130).

But the vanguards of the language in England were not prepared to relinquish their authority for maintaining the purity of English. They felt that the standards of the language were established in England and should be protected from the atrocities of American English, what they viewed as "barbarous" language that would eventually destroy the purity of the English language. In a diary that he kept during his trip to America in 1839, Captain Frederick Marryat provides an opinion that represented those of the British purists:

> . . . it is remarkable how very debased the language has become in a short period in America. . . .
>
> The upper classes of Americans do not . . . speak or pronounce English according to our standards; they appear to have no exact rule to guide them . . . . (quoted in Mathews, 132)

Poet-critic Charles Prentiss was more condemnatory in 1800 in stating that the "laws of English Prosody [had been] settled by Dryden and Pope" and that changes in the language, particularly those brought about by Indian place names, Negro dialects, and the intermingling of racially diverse immigrants, were "gross corruptions" (quoted in Spencer, 37).

But American writers were not deterred. As the fight for political independence escalated and eventually succeeded in the 1770s, writers waged their own battles against the "rough, sonorous diction" of British English, the "turgid stile" and the "purple glare" of British writers, and the self-righteousness and indignation of those people in Great Britain who believed that the standards of the English language could only be established in England, guarded in England, and changed in England (quoted in Spencer, 53).

Though most writers in America after the war agreed that the country needed to break linguistically from Britain, their opinions varied as to the best way to accomplish that. Many concurred with John Adams that "language . . . influences not only the form of government, but the temper, the sentiments, and manners of the people" (Adams, 249), but some were willing to wait for the language to evolve naturally, to change by itself in addressing the unique challenges in a new world. That was Thomas Jefferson's attitude, an attitude shared by others such as Joseph Dennie and Timothy Dwight. In 1801, Dennie predicted that changes in the English language would occur naturally and unavoidably, not due to a patriotic or nationalistic surge towards linguistic freedom but because "images and expressions, which however pertinent in Italy or England, are most ridiculous, when associated with description of our own *home-bred* nature" (quoted in Spencer, 55). Thirty years later, Dwight expressed a similar attitude in writing that American writers should "imitate the style of the best ancient orators, poets, and historians . . . by saying what they would have said if they had been like us, and in our places" (quoted in Spencer, 83). In other words, Americans were to develop an "American" way of using the language, but that development need not come about through antagonistic nationalism or belligerent anti-British feelings. The language would produce its own changes, develop its own "Americanness" naturally, without the need for specific or sustained effort from its writers to institute immediate or artificial changes.

Some writers agreed in general with Jefferson's views concerning language change in America, but they saw the need or the practicality of maintaining certain standards of the language as established in England. John Quincy Adams, certainly a man with influence, favored *eventual* changes in the language, especially through the infusion of new terms necessitated by the unique conditions people faced in the United States. But he agreed with Dennie that there was "a special literary diction established in England to which an American writer was obliged to conform" (quoted in Spencer, 58). Likewise, Benjamin Franklin felt that Americans should not completely abandon the standards of the language, despite the obvious need for the language to conform to the needs of the people in the new country. In a letter to David Hume written after the revolutionary war, he eloquently pleaded the case, seeking British understanding while justifying the American cause:

> The introducing new words, where we are already possessed of old ones sufficiently expressive, I confess must be generally wrong, as it tends to change the language; yet, at the same time, I can not but wish the usage of our tongue permitted making new words, when we want them, by composition of old ones whose meanings are already well understood. . . . Many of our present English words were originally so made; . . . In point of clearness, such compound words would have the advantage of any we can borrow from the ancient or from foreign languages. . . . But I hope with you, that we shall always in America make the best English of [the] Island our standard, and I believe it will be so. (quoted in Bruce, 439-40)

Franklin seems to be straddling the fence here, wanting to argue the logic behind linguistic change in America, but not wanting to accomplish it at the expense of offending his British compeers. Such a position was seen by others as a sign of weakness or uncertainty, but Franklin's attitude was an understandable compromise between his American patriotism and the affection he had developed for England and its people during the many years he lived there.

However, many writers could not go along with such a conciliatory position. They foresaw linguistic independence being achieved only through a complete break from the British in matters of usage, standards, vocabulary, and writing. They saw no way for Americans to gain freedom in the use of their own language if they continued to seek guidance from foreign lands.

The most persistent voice calling for a complete post-revolution break from England came from Noah Webster, who devoted much of his life to defining and describing the English language. In 1789, his *Dissertations on the English Language* issued a plea that was the basis for his early work in establishing an American English:

> As an independent nation, our honor requires us to have a system of our own, in language as well as in government. Great Britain, whose children we are, and whose language we speak, should no longer be *our* standard; for the taste of her writers is already corrupted, and her language on the decline. But if it were not so, she is at too great a distance to be our model, and to instruct us in the principles of our own tongue. (20-21)

In an article published in *The American Magazine* in 1787, he stated his views more emphatically:

> Americans, unshackle your minds and act like independent beings. You have been children long enough, subject to the control, and subservient to the interest, of a haughty parent. . . . [Y]ou have an empire to raise and support by your exertions, and a national character to establish and extend by your wisdom and virtues. . . . [It is] dishonorable to waste life in mimicking the follies of other nations and basking in the sunshine of foreign glory. (*On Being American*, 92)

Webster believed that a language's growth was organic, that no man could obstruct that growth by establishing artificial standards or arbitrary rules. He saw linguistic change and growth as being "rooted in the human mind and the environment" (Moss, 93). Thus, he insisted that no standards, not even those established by the purists in England, could be expected to rein in the language of the new nation, for "a living language admits of no fixed state" (Webster, *Compendious Dictionary*, 101). He also contended that few true Americanisms existed, that all words (even those considered low or colloquial) belonged in the language (and thus in his dictionary).

Webster's actions seemed to contradict his words. In arguing for linguistic freedom from England, he insisted that, since language was alive and constantly changing, it could not be subject to laws that forced it to conform to an artificial standard, but his main goal during his early career was to become recognized across the country (but especially in New England) as "the schoolmaster of America" (Moss, 24). Thus, he wrote spellers and grammar books that broke with British standards, but did so by establishing new rules (i.e. standards) for American English, rules that were usually based on the language as spoken in New England. Thus, he displayed a basic contradiction in his philosophy of language: he argued the futility of trying to conform to standards while, at the same time, he tried to establish his own preferences (based on the dialect of his region) as the new standard.

One reason for Webster's contradictory views is that he saw unity as the strongest force available in fending off British influence. Therefore, even though he himself argued that language is organic, he saw the need for linguistic unity in America, and such a unity translated into establishing norms for everyone to follow. He thought the language was too important to be left "to parents and nurses, to ignorance and caprice, to custom, accident, or nothing," for, if that were to happen, "every person will claim a right to pronounce most agreably [sic] to his own fancy, and the language will be exposed to perpetual fluctuation" (quoted in Moss, 30). One of Webster's main goals was to provide a regularity (not *the* standard) to the pronunciation, spelling, and usage of the English language.

Perhaps Webster's nationalistic approach to the language was necessary to hasten the linguistic break from England. But eventually, he recognized some of the weaknesses in his position and changed it to reflect the maturation of his thought. In 1824, he went to Europe to research materials not available in America. But his trip had another very important goal. Webster went seeking common ground between the languages of America and of England in order to make his work more authoritative and more complete. Webster's friend Samuel Goodrich recalled thinking, upon first seeing Webster in England, that Webster "had come to Europe to perfect his Dictionary!" (quoted in Warfel, 354). Forty years after the publication of his *Dissertations*, the preface to his 1828 edition of *An American Dictionary of the English Language* articulated his altered position:

> It is not only important, but in a degree necessary, that the people of this country should have an *American Dictionary of the English Language*; for, although the body of the language is the same as in England, and it is desirable to perpetuate that sameness, yet some differences must exist. Language is the expression of ideas; and if the people of one country can not preserve an identity of ideas, they cannot retain an identity of language. . . . [T]he genuine English idiom is as well preserved by the unmixed English of this country as it is by the best *English* writers . . . . It is true that many of our writers have neglected to cultivate taste and the embellishments of style; but even these have written the language in its genuine *idiom*. (xii)

As he became better informed and as his nationalistic fervor of the post-revolution era became moderated by a more mature outlook, Webster recognized the need to focus on the similarities between British and American English. Perhaps his conciliatory mood was initiated by the realization that a complete linguistic break from England was neither realistic nor even desirable. Or maybe it was motivated by a genuine desire to make his dictionary a more universal document of "world" English. As pointed out in an article co-authored by Gilbert Youmans and Greg Stratman about America's linguistic break from England, "[D]uring Webster's lifetime, his dictionary was outsold in America by BE [British English] dictionaries and by American dictionaries based on BE models" (146). Nonetheless, Webster's work was generally acknowledged as the most accurate, complete, and scholarly dictionary of the English language ever produced. In 1856, *The Imperial Dictionary* was published in London. Its editor, John Ogilvie, unhesitatingly praised Webster in the preface:

> Webster's dictionary, which forms the basis of the present work, is acknowledged both in this country and in America to be not only superior to either of the two former, but to every other dictionary hitherto published. It is more copious in its vocabulary, more correct in its definitions, more comprehensive in its plan, and in the etymological department it stands unrivaled. (ii)

However, Webster was still not totally captured by this new perspective. Later in the 1828 preface, his argumentative edge returns, and he explains that some terms that originated in England

> . . . are no part of our present language, -- and they cannot be, for the things which they express do not exist in this country. They can be known to us only as obsolete or as foreign words. On the other hand, the institutions in this country which are new and peculiar, give rise to new terms or to new applications of old terms, unknown to the people of England; which cannot be explained by them and which will not be inserted in their dictionaries, unless copied from ours. (xii)

Those comments helped the people in America to realize that "nativeness" in language was desirable, that the so-called standards of the English language as established in Great Britain were not inviolable universals but merely the result and extension of what Edward T. Channing, Professor of Rhetoric at Harvard, called in 1816 "a particular cultural temper and epoch" (quoted in Spencer, 82). In other words, the rules governing the English language in Great Britain were representative only of the place and time of their formulation. And since America was a new and different place in its infancy, it should be allowed to develop its own language apart from that of England.

In the preface to the 1856 edition of Webster's dictionary, the editor, Chauncey A. Goodrich, offers an extended illustration of the inevitability of change focusing on spelling, specifically the BE spellings *-our* (as in *honour*) and *-re* (as in *theatre*). Goodrich shows how the changes in spelling in America were logical, predictable, and unstoppable:

> In reference to *Orthography*, some important alterations have been made, but in strict conformity . . . with [Webster's] principles on this subject. . . . His main principle was, *that the tendencies of our language to greater simplicity and broader analogies, ought to be watched and cherished with the utmost care.* He felt, therefore, that whenever a movement toward wider analogies and more general rules, had advanced so far as to leave but few exceptions to impede its progress, those exceptions ought to be set aside *at once*, and the analogy rendered complete. On this ground he rejected the *u* from such words as *favour*, *labour*, &c. . . . Such, too, is the case with certain terminations in *re*, pronounced *er*; as in *centre*, *metre*, &c. . . .
>
> . . . -- These changes . . . have met with far more favor from the public, than was reasonably to be expected. Most of them have been extensively adopted in our country. They are gaining ground daily, as the reasons by which they are supported are more generally understood; and it is confidently believed that, being founded in established analogies, and intended merely to repress irregularities and remove petty exceptions, they must ultimately prevail. (viii-ix)

The significance of Webster's dictionary in this debate can not be overstated. As Youmans and Stratman explain, Webster's intent to "treat American vocabulary and usage as standard rather than deviant" (149) was the most important of Webster's multiple influences. The end result, as Youmans and Stratman indicate, was that his dictionary "not only established Webster as *the* authority upon American usage, but also led Americans to accept AE [American English] as an independent branch of the language" (149).

As the passages quoted in this chapter indicate, opinions about the nature of the English language and its usage both in England and in America varied greatly not only in content but in justification, purpose, and methodology. Almost everyone agreed that the language would become American, but when, why, and how it would were in question.

As the nineteenth century progressed towards its midpoint, America's writers turned their attention to aspects of this debate that more directly affected them -- the development of an American English to help them produce a uniquely American literature.

Perhaps the initial call for a distinctly American *literature* -- an accomplishment to be gained only through the development of an American *language* -- came from John Neal, who began writing in the late 1810's. He wrote a series of papers for *Blackwood's Magazine* in 1824-1825, published under the title *American Writers* in 1937 edited by Fred L. Pattee. These papers were a sort of alphabetical chronicle of writers in America, not American writers, for Neal could see little being written that distinguished itself as American. His first paper for *Blackwood's* began in this vein, pulling no punches:

> One is continually hearing, more or less, about American literature, . . . as if there were any such thing in the world as American literature; or any such thing in the United States of North America, as a body of native literature – the production of native writers -- bearing any sort of national character, either of wisdom or beauty . . . or having any established authority, even among the people of the United States. And go where one will, since the apparition of one American writer among us, . . . some half-a-dozen stories and story-books; a little good poetry, (with some very bad poems); four or five respectable, and as many more trumpery novels -- with a book or two about theology -- one is pretty sure to hear the most ridiculous and exaggerated misrepresentations, one way or the other, for or against *American* authorship, as if American authorship (so far as it goes) were anything different from English, Scottish, or Irish authorship; . . . . (*American Writers*, 29)

Pattee claims that Neal "was the first in America to be natural in his diction. . . . that [Neal] could use his native idioms and dare to call a spade a damned shovel" (quoted in *American Writers*, 22). The writing style of the passage above illustrates Neal's approach to literature and its linguistic medium -- blunt, straight-ahead, no-holds-barred. And, again as noted by Pattee, Neal's writing was filled with "Maine Yankeeisms." These are examples Pattee culled from Neal's autobiography:

> I did not know this at the time, or I should have helped him to something he would have been sorry to sup, even with a long-handled spoon.
>
> It was intended for encouragement, like patting a fellow on the back, and preparing him for literary canonization, or it may be, for bolting flapjacks, after a manner peculiar to ourselves.
>
> I was born a coward -- not to be mealy-mouthed – a downright coward.
>
> I then threw the blame on the tailor, who ought to have told him before it was too late; for how should I know that tabby-velvet pantaloons wouldn't bear to be sneezed at -- or in?
>
> The whole country was flooded with shin-plasters. (quoted in *American Writers*, 22)

Throughout the papers in *Blackwood's*, Neal sermonizes about the need for native literature in native language. The best summation of his opinions, however, is offered in the unpublished preface he wrote for his 1828 novel *Rachel Dyer*, in which he bemoans the lack of American literature and pleads for an awakening of American writers to the wonders and validity of the materials -- the *real* materials -- provided on their own soil:

> Now believing as I do, in spite of such overwhelming authority, that a man may have a club-foot, or a hump-back, or even red hair and yet be a good man -- peradventure a great man; that a dwarf with a distorted shape may be a giant in goodness of heart and greatness of temper; and that moral beauty *may* exist where it appears not to have been suspected by the chief critics of our age, and of past ages -- . . . .
>
> . . . I would call the attention of our novel-writers and our novel-readers to what is undoubtedly native and peculiar, in the early history of our Fathers: I would urge them to believe that though there is much to lament in that history, there is nothing to conceal; (iv)

He goes on to explain what prompted him to wage the battle alone:

> Would you know what more than . . . all other things determined me at last? I was an American. I had heard the insolent question of a Scotch reviewer [Sydney Smith], repeated on every side of me by native Americans -- "*Who reads an American Book?*" I could not bear this -- I could neither eat nor sleep till my mind was made up. I reasoned with myself -- I strove hard -- but the spirit within me would not be rebuked. . . There must be but one head, one heart in the plan -- . . . it must be single and simple, . . . must have but one point, and that point must be adamant. Being so it may be turned aside: . . . but if at last, any one of the whole should make any impression whatever upon the foe, or effect any entrance whatever into the sanctity and strength of his tremendous phalanx, then, from that moment, the day is our own. Our literature will begin to wake up, and our pride of country will wake up with it. Those who follow will have nothing to do but *keep* what the folorn [sic] hope, who goes [t]o irretrievable martyrdom if he fail, has *gained*.
>
> Moreover -- who was there to stand by the native American that should go out, haply with a sling and stone, against a tower of strength and the everlasting entrenchments of prejudice? Could he hope to find so much as one of his countrymen, to go with him, or even to bear his shield? Would the Reviewers of America befriend him? No -- they have not courage enough to fight their own battles manfully. No -- they would rather flatter than strike. They negociate [sic] altogether too much -- where blows are wanted, they give words. And the best of our literary champions, would they? No; they would only bewail his temerity, if he were the bold head-

> long creature he should be to accomplish the work; and pity his folly and presumption, if he were any thing else. (ix-x)

Neal singles out two of those "literary champions" he accused of agreeing with him publicly but doing little in their writing to indicate that agreement -- Washington Irving and James Fenimore Cooper, who he claims "have gained just enough popular favor to make them afraid of hazarding one jot or tittle of it, by stepping aside into a new path" (xi).

At the heart of his argument was his belief that the English language, as it took shape on the new continent, was vital and alive -- and the only appropriate tongue for the literature of this country:

> The British are a nation of writers. Their novel-writers are as a cloud. True -- true -- but they still want something which they have not. They want a real American writer – one with courage enough to write in his native tongue. *That* they have not, even at this day. *That* they never had. Our best writers are English writers, not American writers. They are English in every thing they do, and in every thing they say, as authors -- in the structure and moral of their stories, in their dialogue, speech, and pronunciation; yea in the very characters they draw. Not so much as one true Yankee is to be found in any of our native books: hardly so much as one true Yankee phrase. Not so much as one true Indian, though you hardly take up a story on either side of the water now, without finding a red-man stowed away in it; and what sort of a red-man? Why one that uniformly talks the best English the author is capable of -- . . . .
>
> . . . For my own part I do not pretend to write English – that is, I do not pretend to write what the English themselves call English -- I do not, and I hope to God . . . that I never shall write what is now worshipped under the name of *classical* English. It is no natural language -- it never was -- it never will be spoken alive on this earth: and therefore, ought never to be written. We have dead languages enough now; but the deadest language I ever met with or heard of, was that in use among writers of Queen Anne's day. (xv)

Adamant and arrogant, Neal failed to have much effect with such doctrinal statements or with his novels. But he was perhaps the first to attempt to write fiction in American English.

Washington Irving, whom Neal singled out to criticize, shared Neal's distaste for using "standard" English as the basis for developing American literature:

> We would rather hear our victories celebrated in the merest doggerel that sprang from native invention, than beg, borrow, or steal from others, the

> thoughts and words in which to express our exaltation. By tasking our own powers, and relying entirely on ourselves, we shall gradually improve and rise to poetical independence . . . . (quoted in Spencer, 27)

Despite Neal's claims that they were not American, James Fenimore Cooper's novels were among the first fictional attempts to depict the people, land, and circumstances (if not the language) of the United States. Cooper shared Neal's desire for American independence in literature and language, but he realized the difficulties involved: "[I]t is much easier to declare war, and gain victories in the field, and establish a political independence, than to emancipate the mind" (quoted in Spencer, 78).

As early as 1828, the same year Webster's dictionary and Neal's *Rachel Dyer* both appeared, Cooper predicted that "in another generation or two far more reasonable English will be used in this country than exists here now. . . . I think it will be just as much the desire of England then to be in our fashion as it was our desire twenty years ago to be in hers" (Mencken, *American Language*, 68). The error in his thinking at that time was that, in 1828, the popularity of BE had certainly not disappeared. Ten years later, in "The American Democrat," Cooper tried to position himself as the American authority on what was and was not acceptable in English. But as with some of his contemporaries, his strategy for claiming an American English countered the desired ends.

Cooper recognized the fact that the language of literature had to speak to the common man; that is, it had to *be* the language of the common man in order for the literature to be genuinely American. His novel *The Prairie* includes the character Obed Battius. Battius is a "pompous naturalist" and a "useless person" who "exemplifies a foolish, academic approach to nature" (Magill, 143). Dr. Battius (or Batt, as he is more commonly known) often has trouble communicating with the less educated "folk" by whom he is surrounded. After a few conversations during which he is frequently misunderstood, he admits, "I must speak in the vernacular, to be comprehended" (156). However, Cooper was unsuccessful in his attempt to "speak the vernacular." Since few (if any) writers before him ever tried to write in the vernacular, he was on his own in trying to render the language of the common man in his writing. Nonetheless, his was a first step on the road to literary independence.

James Russell Lowell saw language as the most vital element of literature, and he insisted that the written language be kept alive to grow and to change along with the spoken language. He saw a living language as one that "is still hot from the hearts and brains of a people, not hardened yet, but moltenly ductile to new shapes of sharp and clear relief in the moulds of new thought" (*Writings of Lowell*, v. 3, 6). He rejected the purist attitudes that written English must forever conform to standards established in England, for he believed that the language was alive and that "its being alive is all that gives it poetic value" (*Writings of Lowell*, v. 3, 220). In the introduction to *The Biglow Papers* (Second Series), he discusses the language of his own writings and insists that the living language was the most appropriate vehicle for literature:

> It had long seemed to me that the great vice of American writing and speaking was a studied want of simplicity, that we were in danger of coming to look on our mother-tongue as a dead language, to be sought in the grammar and dictionary rather than in the heart, and that our only chance of escape was by seeking it at its living sources among those who were "divinely illiterate." . . . Whether it be want of culture, for the highest outcome of that is simplicity, or for whatever reason, it is certain that very few American writers or speakers wield their native language with the directness, precision, and force that are common as the day in the mother country. We use it like Scotsmen, not as if it belonged to us, but as if we wished to prove that we belonged to it, by showing our intimacy with its written rather than its spoken dialect. And yet all the while our popular idiom is racy with life and vigor and originality, bucksome . . . to our new occasions, and proves itself no mere graft by sending up new suckers from the old root in spite of us. It is only from its roots in the living generations of men that a language can be reinforced with fresh vigor for its needs; . . . That we should all be made to talk like books is the danger with which we are threatened . . . . No language after it has faded into diction, none that cannot suck up the feeding juices secreted for it in the rich mother-earth of common folk, can bring forth a sound and lusty book. True vigor and heartiness of phrases do not pass from page to page, but from man to man. Language is the soil of thought, . . . the slow deposit of ages, the shed of foliage of feeling, fancy and imagination, ... There is death in the dictionary; and where language is too strictly limited by convention, the ground for expression to grow in is limited also; . . . . (*Writings*, v. 3, 214),

Lowell often cited William Shakespeare as a prominent example of a writer who readily and easily wrote with the living language of the common man: "If he has need of all the service of what is called a low word, he takes it, ... His pen ennobled them all" (*Writings*, v. 3, 170). He argued that Shakespeare was able to do so because he was writing at the beginning of the modern period of the English language, and "his medium was an uninhibited young language which logicians and grammarians had not yet shackled with proscriptive and prescriptive rules in an attempt at standardization" (quoted in Harder, 180).

He also cited Abraham Lincoln as a more contemporary and American example of an exemplary style:

> President Lincoln, the only really great public man whom these latter days have seen, was great also in this, that he was master -- witness his speech at Gettysburg -- of a truly masculine English, classic because it was of no special period, and level at once to the highest and lowest of his countrymen. (*Writings*, v. 3, 214)

Like Cooper, Lowell could not rely on models for writing in the colloquial language of America; he had to rely on his own knowledge and experience with the language and the people. And his results were more successful than Cooper's. Lowell's colloquial writings, best exemplified by *The Biglow Papers* (which H. L. Mencken described as the first masterpiece of American colloquial and national literature) helped to define what American literature was to be and how language could (or should) play a role. In these writings, he displayed an American writing style, one that relied on the depiction of regional variations in vocabulary, grammar, and pronunciation (Harder, 184). However, as Mencken points out, Lowell's non-dialect writing was not nearly as distinctive:

> His writing in his own person, however, showed but little sign of [American colloquialism]: he gradually adopted a very effective prose style, but it did not differ materially from that of his New England contemporaries. (*Supplement*, 130)

Though Lowell achieved a measure of success in undermining the linguistic authority of the British purists, he did so in a way similar to Webster's. He simply shifted the authority of the language from England to New England, specifically the Brahmin Boston of the mid-1880's. Again, such actions were contradictory, though such contradictory behavior was perhaps necessary and inevitable in the fight of American writers to gain control over their language.

In 1855, Charles Astor Bristed was the first American to publish a defense of AE in England. His contribution to *Cambridge Essays* was entitled "The English Language in America." Mencken saw it as "the most intelligent brief discussion of the subject ever printed" (*AL*, 69).

Bristed argued to the British reading public that American English was worthy of study, that it was important and vital "to investigate the course of a great living language, transplanted from its primitive seat, brought into contact and rivalry with other civilized tongues, and exposed to various influences, all having a *prima facie* tendency to modify it" (quoted in Mencken, *AL*, 69).

Bristed confronted the most common objections to American English. He argued that most Americanisms had been derived from BE sources, that AE had developed very few new words, and that "the deviations from standard English which occur in America are fewer and less gross than those which may be found in England herself" (Mencken, *AL*, 70).

And then there was Walt Whitman, a writer who rarely failed to resist whatever restraints presented themselves. As for the language of literature, he wrote:

> The forms of grammar are never persistently obeyed, and cannot be.
> The Real Dictionary will give all words that exist in use, the bad words as well as any. --- The Real Grammar will be that which declares itself a nucleus of the spirit of the laws, even by violating them, if necessary. --- The English language is grandly lawless like the race who use it. (6)

Of course, the language was not "lawless" any more than it was permanently fixed; in this seeming overstatement, Whitman meant that the laws were ever changing from person to person, region to region, generation to generation. But popular sentiment rarely embraces that which seems lawless, finding safety and comfort in the tried and true. As Van Wyck Brooks explains:

> Literary English with us is a tradition, just as Anglo-Saxon law is a tradition. They persist not as the normal expressions of a race, . . . but through prestige and precedent and the will and habit of a dominating class largely out of touch with a national fabric . . . . (*Coming of Age*, 8)

But American writers, from Webster to Whitman, recognized the cost of maintaining such a tradition -- the inability to break completely from Britain, the difficulty of establishing an American literature, the impossibility of presenting the native stuff of this land in their writing.

By the 1860's, nearly one-hundred years after America gained political independence, the struggle for literary independence was still going on. Although many writers had called for and justified the development of an American English as the true voice of the people in America and as the only appropriate medium for their literature, the struggle was neither consistent nor unified. Then William Dean Howells appeared on the American literary scene. An outsider from the Midwest, Howells infiltrated the Brahmin literary inner circle and eventually became one of the most influential literary figures in this country. His interest in language involved him in the struggle to break free from British standards, but because he was from the Midwest, he resisted (usually) the linguistic authority of New England, as well, though his commentary often wavered between his insistence on the use of "real" language (his descriptivism) and his desire for an effective use of the language (his prescriptivism). These two warring impulses will be illustrated in the next chapter. But his primary focus was on language, the language of literature. So nearly one hundred years after the country had achieved its political independence, the country's language -- *American* English -- finally had its most ardent and influential proponent.

CHAPTER 3

Howells on Language

Be plain as you please;
there is nothing better than homespun.
Howells to Hamlin Garland, 1897

In the late 1860's, when Howells assumed the editorship of *The Atlantic Monthly*, his mere presence there was a harbinger of change in the literature of America. As the first non-New Englander to hold such a prestigious literary position in this country, he provided a perspective with a more national scope. That perspective prompted him to advocate significant changes in both the content and the form of literature. The primary change he advocated in literary content was based on his belief that literature should focus on the everyday realities of the life of the common man (including those common folk in regions other than New England). In order for such changes to be effective, lasting, and realistic, Howells knew, as did many of his literary predecessors discussed in the preceding chapter, that the *language* of literature had to change, as well. Thus, he consistently emphasized the importance of language in the development of a realistic literature.

In over fifty years of writing -- in editorials, criticism, essays, and correspondence -- Howells displayed a fascination with language, both in its everyday use and in its role in literature. He commented on dialect, grammar, vocabulary, pronunciation, euphemisms, contractions, spelling, etymology, and punctuation. He also participated in debates regarding British and American English, prescriptive vs. descriptive grammar, and standard and vernacular usage. In addition, his reviews of literary works (by his predecessors as well as by his contemporaries) often focused on their use of language. Howells had the heart and soul of a linguist, and his preoccupation with language was ever-present.

Howells's correspondence was everywhere sprinkled with comments on language, from prescriptive reprimands of siblings to descriptive notes to his colleagues about curiosities. The following excerpts illustrate the variety of subjects and recipients of his correspondence:

November 1859, to his sisters, Anne and Aurelia – depicting the speech of a German editor with whom he was acquainted:

. . . I was gome of a refolutionary vamily. . . . My little girl, ven I deech dem do her – she veeped. (*Selected Letters*, v. 1, 50)

September 1860, to his sister, Anne Howells:

If you conclude to write me in the French, have the goodness to spell the name of that language with a capital 'F'; and not again to say you are 'studying' anything. It is quite as bad to say 'rebublican' . . . . (*SL*, v. 1, 63)

February 1860, to his father, William C. Howells:

Elinor is quite Yankee enough to know what 'snug weather' means. At present she's devoting most of her faculties to achieve some idea of the letter R as pronounced by correct speakers of English, and I've been trying to teach her to say *toad*, though I'm ashamed to add she's done nothing better than *to-ed* as yet. (*SL*, v. 1, 138)

September 1865, to aspiring author Don L. Wyman:

There are many felicities of expression, and much poetic feeling in the "Onion and the Dolphin," which the editors of the *Atlantic* must have seen;

. . . There are licenses of diction in it, which no one should permit himself, and the author's knowledge of the Latin sources of many words is too apparent; it is scarcely worth while to puzzle the English reader, in order to afford the classic scholar a doubtful pleasure. (*SL*, v. 1, 225-26)

December 1874, to writer Edmund C. Stedman:

Yu shal hav the Wuster spelling of cors, if yu lik. For my on part, I so detest al idl and unecesary leters in riting, that I wud wilingly banish them from print, ... (*SL*, v. 2, 80)

December 1874, to writer Belton O. Townsend:

. . . [T]here is but one precept in such matters: say out simply, distinctly, directly what you have to say. (*SL*, v. 2, 83)

December 1875, to James Russell Lowell:

What mostly "stumps" me in this English tongue . . . is the wills and shalls, and woulds and shouldn'ts. Their true use comes only from being born in one or the other of the Englands. (*SL*, v. 2, 114)

August 1877, to Belton O. Townsend:

[T]he simplest word is the best. (*SL*, v. 2, 171)

October 1881, to George W. Cable:

. . . [T]he Nancanou ladies . . . . Oh the charm of their English! We speak nothing else now but that dialect. . . . [T]he last chapter, exquisite -- that woman left a sweet taste in my mouth; Honore', with his guttaral *r's* noble and charming; . . . . (*SL*, v. 2, 297)

June 1883, to his father, depicting the accent of Welsh English:

Many a time 'e's trod this path, sir. Many's the 'alf crown I've 'ad from 'im, sir. (*SL*, v. 3, 71)

September 1885, to Samuel Clemens:

Did you ever read Defoe's Roxana? If not, then read it, not merely for some of the deepest insights into the lying, suffering, sinning, well-meaning human soul, but the best and most natural English that a book was ever written in. (*SL*, v. 3, 127)

January 1888, to George Bainton:

I should advise any beginner to study the raciest, strongest, best spoken speech, and let the printed speech alone: that is, try to write straight from the thought, without bothering about the manner, except to conform to the spirit or genius of the language. I once thought Latinized diction was to be avoided; now I think Latinized syntax is to be guarded against. (*SL*, v. 3, 213)

September 1888, to Thomas W. Higginson:

I was wrong to let a New Englander use 'fool' adjectively, but I couldn't resist the color it promised to give; it's a tint of my native Southern Ohio parlance. (*SL*, v. 3, 227)

May 1894, to Higginson:

[T]here is good literary English, and there is good natural English. . . . I will confess that I prefer the good natural English; and, confessing this, I will add that what I remember to have said to Mr. Johnson was that I did not find the participial construction natural English. . . . [I]t is better to write . . . as simply as we speak, unless . . . we speak as formally as we write. (*SL*, v. 4, 66-67)

January 1897, to Hamlin Garland:

You have got some newspaper diction in your pen-point, and you must shake it out. You are so good that you can afford to say things with the distinction they deserve from the best. Here and there a word, a phrase jarred on me. Be plain as you please; there is nothing better than homespun; but the clothing-store is no place for your thoughts to dress themselves. (*SL*, v. 4, 139)

February 1902, to Henry James:

Mrs. Jasper was a most beautiful creature – out of Western New York, I should think from the way she broke through into her native R's (from the English accent which the school cultivates) in moments of high excitement. (*SL*, v. 5, 14)

March 1902, to Thomas Bailey Aldrich:

If you ever treat me like that again, I will belt you over the muns, as that unknown friend of yours said long ago in New York when even the tough spoke classic English. (*SL*, v. 5, 16)

December 1904, to Stedman:

Poor Harry Harland is here, lung-sick; but his doctor, a delightful Englishman, tells me he will 'pull round.' Of course he means 'through,' but you can't expect an Englishman to speak our language correctly. (*SL*, v. 5, 115)

November 1906, to his brother Joseph A. Howells:

For heaven's sake look to your grammar! Hot on my scolding you write 'John and his stomach does.' Would you write 'The boys does?' John and his stomach are just as plural. (*SL*, v. 5, 196)

October 1912, to Albert B. Paine:

At times it grovels in mere newspaper parlance. How can you . . . write 'as does'? What do you mean by an 'ill man'? I suppose, a sick man; but an 'ill man' is a bad man. (*SL*, v. 6, 23)

February 1914, to Leo F. Hartman:

I was going to reproach you for writing 'queried Poole, reflectively,' and 'quoted Evelyn in a stage whisper,' and 'protested the man,' and the like; but reading over *Silas Lapham* just now I found that I had done the same thirty years ago. Still those inversions are not modern, and they were always ungainly. (*SL*, v. 6, 48)

Howells's earliest formal comments on language were also among his earliest critical comments to appear in print. In 1866, in *The Nation*, he discussed the use of euphemisms and the "true" meaning of words used by politicians. In those brief comments, Howells displayed his ability to recognize the effects of language that are used to mask the true intentions of speakers. That commentary was his first of hundreds in American literary journals about the English language, commentaries that displayed the wide scope of his interest in and his knowledge of linguistic matters.

Later that year, he was hired as the assistant editor of *The Atlantic Monthly* and began a long and distinguished career as a reviewer. He reviewed literary and non-literary works, often basing his opinions of a work on the author's use of language:

Lowell's *The Biglow Papers* (January 1867)

We enjoy . . . such glimpses as the author chooses to give us of his purpose in writing the Biglow papers, and in adopting the Yankee dialect for his expression, as well as of his methods of studying this dialect. . . . [I]t is effortless, familiar talk with his readers, always significant, but persistent in nothing, and in tone as full and rich as the best talk of Montaigne or Cervantes.

C. G. Leland's *Han's Breitmann's Party* (October 1868)

It's [sic] instrument is not a dialect or patois characterizing a race or locality, but merely the broken English of the half-American German.

Louisa May Alcott's *An Old-Fashioned Girl* (June 1870)

There's some humor in it, and as little pathos as possible, and a great deal of sense, but also some poor writing, and some bad grammar.

Harriett Beecher Stowe's *Oldtown Fireside Stories* (March 1872)

. . .[[T]he Yankee talk . . . is always glib and easy, and suggests the life of an old provincialized community, with its settled order and its intimacy and familiarity.

. . . [T]he talk of Sam Lawson . . . can only come from the naturalness of first-rate art.

Edward Eggleston's *The Circuit Rider* (June 1874)

[He] placed an inartistic stress upon unimportant details of dialect, customs and character.

F.H. Underwood's *Lord of Himself* (September 1874)

These poor whites seem to us the most artistically managed people in the book; their dialect is faithfully caught, and the grotesque squalor of their life is graphically sketched.

Abley Sage Richardson's *The History of Our Country* (August 1875)

Now and then she makes the mistake of dragging into her well-behaved diction some phrase of doubtful taste, caught from our slang-poisoned vernacular, and here and there we are sorry to see that she has trouble with the preterits [sic] of such difficult verbs as lie and plead. . . ; generally the style is good American-English, -- the only kind of English that Americans can be expected to write 'like natives'.

Stowe's *We and Our Neighbors* (August 1875)

The way in which the parties . . . habitually address each other is quite intolerable when we consider that they profess to represent very good elements of our society.

Sarah Orne Jewett's *Deephaven* (June 1877)

> [T]he talk of the people is rendered with a delicious fidelity.

Thomas R. Lounsbury's *History of the English Language* (March 1880)

> [Praises] the author's unpedantic and healthful manner of looking upon the language as an expression of national life, not as an ingenious piece of mechanism constructed for the amusement of grammarians.

In the late 1880's and early 1890's, as editor of *Harper's*, Howells maintained a focus on language as an important element in evaluating the merits of literature. He praised the writing of Ulysses S. Grant for its "peculiar, almost plebeian, plainness" (August 1886). He loved the poetry of the Norwegian poet Bjornstjerne Bjornson because he had "refreshed [the poetry] from the never-failing springs of the common speech" (February 1889).

But the one review that provides the best insight into Howells's attitude on the English language was the one he wrote on Richard Grant White's *Words and their Uses, Past and Present: A Study of the English Language*. White's work had a great impact on Howells's own thinking. Echoes and reiterations of White can be heard from Howells following the publication of White's book. These passages are from White, yet they sound remarkably like Howells:

> Usage in the end makes language; determining not only the meaning of words, but their suggestiveness, and also their influence. For the influence of man upon language is reciprocated by the influence of language upon man; and the mental tone of a community may be vitiated by a yielding to the use of loose, coarse, low and frivolous phraseology. (4-5)

> Language is generally formed by indirect and unconscious effort; but when a language is subjected to the constant action of such degrading influences as those which threaten ours, it may be well to introduce into its development a little consciousness. . . . [M]an's language, like man himself, grows by a gradual accretion of trifles . . . . (6)

> Language is rarely corrupted, and is often enriched, by the simple, unpretending, ignorant man, who takes no thought of his parts of speech. (6)

> Language is made for man, and not man for language; but yet no man, no number of men, however great, can of purpose change the meaning of one monosyllable. (12)

> Usage . . . is not, as it is often claimed to be, the absolute law of language; and it never has been so with any people -- could not be, or we should have an example of a language which had not changed from what it was in its first stage.
>
> . . . [T]he authority of general usage . . . is not absolute in language. There is a misuse of words which can be justified by no authority, however great, by no usage, however general. (24)

> The right use of words is not a matter to be left to pedants and pedagogues. It belongs to the daily life of every man. The misuse of words confuses ideas, and impairs the value of language as a medium of communication. . . . The power of language to convey one man's thoughts and purposes to another, is in direct proportion to a common consent as to the meaning of words. (80)

In commenting on White's book, Howells wrote what came to be his guiding principle regarding the language of literature:

> The English language is primarily in the mouths of living men; it has no transmissible life but what comes thence, and there we must seek it if we would say anything clearly or stoutly to our generation. (*AM*, March 1871)

That statement summarizes Howells's theory of realistic literary language, that language is the *creation* of *living* speakers and that its forms can never be fixed. But as the passages quoted so far in this chapter indicate, Howells's commentary is (or seems to be) contradictory. He proclaims that the language is "primarily in the mouths of living men," and he praises the "well springs of common speech." But he also labels the vernacular "slang-poisoned" and criticizes writers for slips of grammar and diction based on popular usage rather than on proper grammar and usage. As the scope and importance of his career increased during the next decade, these seeming contradictions did not disappear.

In his first "Editor's Study" for *Harper's* magazine (January 1886), Howells provided his first extended commentary on language (perhaps *treatise* would be a more accurate word). This lengthy discussion is an important summation of Howells's linguistic theory for literature, so an extended section has been quoted here, with interspersed comments (in italics) on some of the contradictions in his analysis:

> . . . we hope that our inherited English may be constantly freshened and revived from the native sources which literary decentralization will help to keep open, and we will own that as we turned over those novels coming from Philadelphia, from New Mexico, from rural New England, from New York, every local flavor of diction gave us courage and pleasure.

Here, Howells calls for authors to present regional varieties of English in their works in order to provide realistic language from the mouths of their characters, as well as in their own narratives. He seems to advocate "literary decentralization," though other comments illustrate that he has no qualms in assuming and maintaining his position of literary arbiter.

> . . . no language is ever old on the lips of those who speak it, no matter how decrepit it drops from the pen. We have only to leave our studies, editorial and other, and go into the shops and fields . . . ; and from the beginning Realism, before she had got a name or put on her capital letter, had divined this near-at-hand truth along with the rest. Mr. Lowell, the greatest and finest realist who ever wrought in verse, showed us that . . . he heard Yankee farmers talk;

This further emphasizes his call for the representation of regional English. It is interesting to note that Howells claims that those who focus on "studies" -- including editors -- should leave behind what might be called "Book English" and listen to the common people around them to hear the language as it should be depicted in fiction.

> and without asking that our novelists of the widely scattered centres shall each seek to write in his local dialect, we are glad . . . of every tint any of them gets from the parlance he hears; it is much better than the tint he will get from the parlance he reads.

Here Howells discourages writers from consistently presenting their own local dialects in their narratives. He seems to be calling for a measured and readable representation of dialect -- or parlance -- that the writers have heard from other people.

> One need not invite slang into the company of its betters, though perhaps slang has been dropping its *s* and becoming language ever since the world began, and is certainly sometimes delightful and forcible beyond the reach of a dictionary.

That is the prescriptive side of Howells coming out. He discourages the use of slang in literature, though he also admits that slang is a vital force that makes the language alive and ever-changing.

> We would not have any one go about for new words, but if one of them came aptly, not to reject its help.

Howells seems to seek a middle ground here (like Franklin did) in discouraging the coining of new words but expressing his willingness to accept them, when such new terms are needed.

> For our novelists to try to write Americanly, from any motive, would be a dismal error, but being born Americans, we would have them use "Americanisms" whenever these serve their turn; and when their characters speak, we should like to hear them speak true American, with all the varying Tennesseean, Philadelphian, Bostonian, and New York accents.

Howells does not think authors should deliberately set out to write "Americanly," but that they should just allow their writing to flow naturally as they themselves use it. This statement shows Howells's belief that writers could and should develop a natural style -- an American style -- while at the same time encouraging them to give their characters regional speech. His concept of an American writing style seems to revolve around the use of Americanisms. And he recognizes that the vast majority of Americanisms are derived locally and regionally rather than nationally.

> If we bother ourselves to write what the critics imagine to be "English," we shall be priggish and artificial, and still more so if we make our Americans talk "English." There is also this serious disadvantage about "English," that if we wrote the best "English" in the world, probably the English themselves would not know it, or, if they did, certainly would not own it.

Howells sees naturalness as a most desirable trait in the language of literature. And he contends that the only way American writers can sound natural is to write American English. He also is intimating that British writers do not use the language in the standard way that their critics seem to think. He uses that argument as a basis for justifying the development of a native American style of writing by using the language to suit American needs.

> It has always been supposed by grammarians and purists that a language can be kept as they find it; but languages, while they live, are perpetually changing. God apparently meant them for the common people . . . ; and the common people will use them freely as they use other gifts of God. On their lips our continental English will differ more and more from the insular English, and we believe that this is not deplorable, but desirable.

He jabs at the notion of grammarians and prescriptivists who think the language can be guarded and protected from change. Howells knows that language inevitably changes, and he calls for and supports the natural development of the language. He also realizes that the majority of the changes that take place come from the common people.

To this point, Howells seems to present himself as a man of inconsistencies and self-contradictions. He obviously is a proponent of simple, natural language. He supports language change and recognizes the fact that the changes are inevitable and will inevitably come from ordinary people. He does not decry that fact; he champions it as the most effective and desirable way for language to change. In addition, he frequently urges writers to use the emerging American style in their writing; in particular, he encourages them to depict appropriate regional varieties of American English in the speech of their fictional characters.

But beneath those attitudes lies a purist strain. Howells wants writers (and non-writers, as well) to use the language correctly. He is irritated by slips of grammar and usage, as is illustrated by passages from his reviews and his personal correspondence. He wants people to use the language properly, but that is not to say that he wants them to use it formally. He understood the differences between proper/improper usage and formal/informal usage, as defined by the country's arbiters of language (who at that time were still all New Englanders). He disliked infractions of proper usage, as well as the unnecessary and unnatural use of formal English. He saw the latter as based on non-native prescriptions that emanated from across the ocean in a land and by a people now foreign to America.

Therefore, Howells's linguistic attitudes were not as contradictory as they at first seem, though he does contradict himself occasionally. Like Noah Webster, he often argues against accepting British English as a standard, arguing that the language in the new country must be allowed to grow organically, free from the confining strictures of England's purist attitudes. However, like Webster, he tended to replace the standards of England with the standards of New England. In some ways, he failed to follow his own call for seeking real language in the mouths of living men. Or, rather, he did seek the language there, but he sometimes was affected by the identity of the living man he was listening to.

Howells followed his lengthy commentary in his first "Editor's Study" with another long discussion about literary language. This editorial illustrates not only the emphasis he placed on the accurate use of language in literature but also his knowledge of dialectal usage. He favors the depiction of dialect in literature, but as a critic and a reader, he expects literary dialects to be accurate and appropriate for their characters:

> It is some such reluctance, perhaps, which renders us sensitive to the compliment lately paid our poor American language by two English novelists. These writers have wished to reproduce the accents and expressions which we commended last month to the attention of our native authors, and they have imagined several American characters entirely for the purpose of having somebody speak American. Our foreign compatriots are not much like the fellow-citizens we know at home, but it can be honestly said of them that they are as like us as their talk is like our untutored speech. We believe it was Mr. Robert Buchanan who, feeling that the language of Shakespeare and Milton would no longer serve as a means of international *rapprochement*, was the first Briton to write in the New England dialect; at any rate he produced a poem in it which he was not able to tell from one of Mr. Lowell's; and now Mr. Black, in his *White Heather*, has a character who speaks perceptible American; only, he is a man, and he speaks young-lady American as often as masculine American. To us the two sorts are distinctive enough, but Mr. Black . . . is not so much to blame for getting them mixed. He makes Mr. Hodson say a London fog is "just too dismal for anything," but we feel that it was his daughter who supplied Mr. Black with that phrase; and when the young lady says, "You bet your pile on that," we suspect that Mr. Black really had the expression from her younger brother.
>
> As for Mr. Grant Allen, who has made a country boy from northern New York the hero of his novel *Babylon*, we should not know exactly where or how he got his Americanisms. (February 1886)

Howells lauds the attempt of British writers to depict the speech of American characters accurately, seeing it as another step towards the linguistic independence so long sought by American writers. But he does not care for the actual language represented, citing examples to illustrate that a writer -- American or not -- must depict speech accurately. As he says, for example, a male character should not speak "young-lady American."

In the following months and years, the pages of *Harper's* issued many more of Howells's comments relating to the realistic usage of language in literature. These comments were often included within discussions and reviews of works by other writers, and his comments continued to focus on his preference for a simple, unaffected, common language. The following excerpts from some of his reviews illustrate how his opinions of a work were often affected by linguistic concerns:

> [Ulysses S. Grant] does not cast about for phrases, but takes the word, whatever it is, that will best give his meaning, as if it were a man or a force of men, for the accomplishment of a feat of arms. There is not a moment wasted in preening and prettifying, after the fashion of literary men; there is no thought of style, and so the style is good as it is in the Book of Chronicles, as it is in *Pilgrim's Progress*, or in a novel of Defoe's, with a peculiar, almost plebeian, plainness at times. (August 1886)

> The young writer who attempts to report the phrase and carriage of every-day life, who tries to tell just how he has heard men talk and seen them look, is made to feel guilty of something low and unworthy by the stupid people who would like to have him show how Shakespeare's men talked and looked, or Scott's, or Thackeray's, or Balzac's, or Hawthorne's, or Dickens' . . . . (December 1887)

> [Bjornson] is one of the chief of those Norsemen of our time who have led their poetry back not only to the life but to the language of the people, and have refreshed it from the never-failing springs of the common speech. (February 1889)

> If the American we speak and write shall incidentally become as different in its vocabulary from the English of the scholasticists as the rehabilitated Norse is from the Danish, we do not think that will be cause for grief, but the contrary. From its grammatical simplicity and inflexibility our language on the imaginative and critical side is always in danger of becoming poverty-stricken; any one who employs it to depict or to characterize finds the phrases thumbed over and worn and blunted with incessant use, and experiences a joy in the bold locutions which these writers report from the lips of the people, where it is still alive. (February 1889)

> Of the English that [H. H. Boyeson] writes so wonderfully the worst that any one could say is that it is too American; and we have no wish to say this. Between book English and spoken English, we prefer the spoken; and we would rather have Mr. Boyeson over-vernacular than pedantic; he would be closer to life. (August 1889)

> [Ironquill's poetry presents] the natural carriage of the-man-let-loose, and the natural language of his let-looseness; though we hasten to reassure the reader that this language which we have called the dialect of life is not a more or less factitious Southwestern parlance, but the ordinary more or less newspaperized English of our day. (April 1890)

> [Lowell's] thoughts flow as naturally in the parlance that he caught from the lips of the wagoners and ploughmen of the rustic village Cambridge once was as in "the language of Shakespeare and Milton": . . . . (June 1891)

> [T]remendous literary upheaval in Norway . . . shattered all the old literary ideals, and sent the poets and novelists of that little, mighty land back to the people to study their language at its source on their lips, and to purify and strengthen their diction for the expression of those conceptions in ethics and aesthetics which the names of Bjornson and Ibsen now stand. (July 1891)

> . . . where our language does differ from that of the mother English, or grandmother English, the critics who wish us to have a national literature are not particularly pleased. They call our differences Americanisms, and they are afraid of their becoming the language of the whole race. (November 1891)

In an 1894 interview with Clifton Johnson, Howells again commented on the need for plainness and simplicity and realism within the dialogue in fiction:

> The time will come when our politest literature will be written and printed with all the contractions that we use in speech. . . . We never say 'do not' -- we say 'don't,' and I think it should so stand in print. The same applies to a good many other words. . . .
>
> . . . One of the most common errors is in the participial – for instance, you would never say, 'Seeing you in the window, I stopped to call.' You would say, 'I saw you and stopped.' Yet most writers have no hesitation in turning such phrases . . . . It really is not English. . . .
>
> If you report conversation, you must make it true to life, and in the main must write it as it would be spoken. Bad grammar and a degree of roughness are not objectionable or offensive, but profanity and coarseness . . . are . . . . (581)

Ten years later, in a 1904 interview with A. Schade van Westrum, Howells reiterated those thoughts:

> Write always as people speak and write, or as nearly as you can. That is part of the realistic theory of fiction. And it is productive of true art in the hands of a master. Did you ever read Defoe's Roxana? . . . It is colloquial, it is written in the spoken tongue of that day. But . . . it is one of the best written novels in the language. (29)

In the mid 1890's, Howells began writing "Life and Letters," a column in *Harper's Weekly*. He continued his emphasis on linguistic topics, but increasingly, he focused on the use of dialect in literature. In the June 8, 1895 issue, Howells provides an extended assessment on the past and present state of dialect in literature. A lengthy section of this editorial is presented here to give the full measure of Howells's words and critical perspective at the time. Again, critical commentary on Howells's views is interspersed.

> It was inevitable that the use of dialect should grow with the wider diffusion of the impulse to get the whole of American life into our fiction. This impulse, partly conscious and partly unconscious, is what has given us the rank we shall be found hereafter to have taken in the literature of our age, and which, whether it has given us great American novels or not, has expressed the national temperament, character, and manner with a fulness [sic] not surpassed by contemporary fiction in the case of any other people.

Howells identifies the popular trend at this time of depicting dialect in literature. He is pleased that literature has taken this course, knowing that he helped chart the way. He also predicts that this realism in the language would come to be seen as the most vital and important aspect of the literature of the day. He admits that this period may not have produced many great novels, but he sees the accomplishments made as being more important. This attitude is interesting in that it forecasts his own future reputation -- he came to be known as a writer who wrote a few good novels but more importantly offered a realistic look at life in his day.

> It may be said to have begun where our literature began, in New England, and Lowell's accurate and exquisite study of the Yankee dialect in the Biglow Papers was the first work of the kind that was truly artistic, or of the effect that I mean. . . .
>
> There is some dialect of the genuine sort in Mrs. Stowe's Oldtown Folks, and Mrs. Rose Terry Cooke had a good ear for Yankee parlance, and reported it delightfully in her New England stories: . . . . Mrs. Phelps Ward has handled it well, and so has Mrs. Prescott Spofford; . . . .

Without turning to one of her books I should not be ready to say whether Miss Jewett employs much dialect or not. I have the impression that she imparts the spirit of Yankee parlance without too much insisting upon the letter; an accent here and there suggests it, and a characteristic phrase gives the touch of color that charms. I have a like impression of Miss Wilkins, but I have the impression too that she actually uses dialect rather more than Miss Jewett does.

. . . The next attempts at dialect among our writers seem to have been made in California, where forms of the Pike found their way into Mr. Bret Harte's stories and poems along with Cockneyisms naturalized out of Dickens. A truer Pike was a little later studied by Mr. John Hay in his ballads; but I do not think that the Southwestern parlance which goes generically by that name has been cultivated much farther in literature. Mr. Cable's ever-delightful use of the Creole accents and forms followed in order of time, I believe, and these remain, to my thinking, almost the most delicately managed of all the experiments in dialect which our prose authors have made. Even with our stupid orthography, which is so false to its offices that it is impossible to write in English the commonest vowel sound of the language so that it cannot be mistaken for some other, though there are half a dozen ways of writing it, Mr. Cable has contrived to spell the speech of his Creole characters so that you know just how they spoke. He had noticed that in a dialect or patois each person permits himself to characterize the common speech, and so he varies the English of one Creole from that of another, and he marks the distinction of white Creole from colored Creole. . . .

Another phase of French-English parlance has been much more recently studied by Mr. William McClennan, in his sketches of Canadian life and character. These are mostly in . . . the speech of a . . . narrator, who is native to the dialect used, and nothing could be more delicate than the perfection with which its peculiarities are touched and turned to the light. . . .

Mr. Cable's performance has been emulated by that of two other writers, like himself Southerners, among whom dialect has been studied with a fresh interest no longer possible in New-Englanders. The two writers I mean are, of course, Mr. Joel Chandler Harris in the Uncle Remus stories and Mr. Thomas Nelson Page in his several sketches of Virginia negro character. I ought also to speak of at least one brief essay in negro dialect by Mark Twain, who in the limits of a little story supposed to be told by an old negress has philosophized it as thoroughly as any of the others.

I do not know of any Southerner who has given the local dialects of the American whites so well as Miss Murfree. As you read you feel sure that those people spoke as she has represented their speech, and that so much of their character dwells in their parlance that if she had made them speak otherwise or less faithfully to their usage, much that is precious would have been lost. . . .

The middle West and the Northwest seem not to have any speech of their own so strongly local that it characterizes the section by a difference from the speech of the East and the South, which colonized with their accents as well as their populations. Yet in Indiana one of the most sensitive of our observers has found a parlance in which he has cast some of the sweetest and finest verse which can be called American. Without the poetry of James Whitcomb Riley our literature would be so much the poorer that it seems idle to state the fact; . . . .

Mr. Hamlin Garland has given us the notion of something native in the vernacular of rural Wisconsin, but the speech of his characters is too largely the speech of the rustic in the West everywhere to be accepted as a distinct variety; and the talk that Mr. Owen Wister is now reporting in his stories of the far West is much the same frontier talk we have been accustomed to in earlier writers. . .

. . . [T]he work done in "tough" New York dialect by the author of the Chimmie Fadden stories . . . had been anticipated by Mr. Stephen Crane in a story called Maggie, a Girl of the Streets, which was printed some years ago, but could not be said to have been published, so wholly did it fail of recognition. There was reason for this in its grim, not to say grimy truth, and in the impossibility to cultured ears of a parlance whose texture is so largely profanity. . . . [B]ut it embodied perhaps the best tough dialect which has yet found its way into print. That dialect has been spoken much longer on the stage in the comedies of Mr. Harrigan, and it may be heard by any listener in the streets of certain quarters of the city. Those who have not studied it, or listened to it attentively, can have little notion how greatly the common pronunciation of our language has been corrupted by the mixture of races in the poorer quarter, and how a whole glossary of new words has sprung up from the rank life of the mixture. . . . I have often heard phrases in the streets of New York which in accent and texture were as strange to me as some whose speakers did not believe themselves to be speaking English.

With this passage, Howells's comments on numerous works by writers who employed dialect illustrate his familiarity with a wide range of works and his knowledge of the subject. These comments again offer an example of how highly he prioritized language as an element of effective literature.

A very pretty argument could be made to prove that the tendency of the English spoken among us is towards heterogeneity, rather than homogeneity, but I am not going to make it, for fear I should be tempted to force some conclusions without the documents.

This comment shows Howells's perceptiveness in linguistic matters in his realization of the nature of American English. It also illustrates his good sense in not attempting to develop an argument without proper, documented support -- though he was not always hesitant to do so.

> But I should really like to say something more of dialect, or rather to account for its use, and justify it. I am not sure that I always like to read it; but I think I should have lost much without some effects which it has accomplished in the representation of our national life;

Howells's comment from the reader's perspective is interesting in that it serves to justify the use of dialect even when it may be disliked by a reader. He sees the effects of realism as taking precedence. That can be interpreted as a writer's indifference or as a critic's preference. It can also be seen as an understandable and predictable opinion of a man who served as both writer and critic.

> and I am sure that the sympathies of every artist in fiction will be with the writers whom a change of the general reader's mood could deprive of one of the great resources of their art, and would leave to show in dry and lifeless paraphrase the racy thought and vital feeling of the characters who naturally express themselves in dialect.

This final comment offers his contention that pressuring writers to avoid dialect in their writing would deprive them of a fundamental and vital device for creating important literature.

Two weeks later, in the June 22 issue, Howells resumed this discussion with another long commentary on dialect and literature (again interspersed with parenthetical observations):

> In reporting dialogue, . . . most writers avail themselves of vernacular usage to give an air of reality to their scene, and write the contractions which we all speak, unless, they are writing romance, when they instinctively feel that the formality of the accepted book-language is more in keeping with the wholly artificial frame. Hawthorne even had his people, or some of them, say Methinks, and they would almost as probably have said Methinks in life, as they would have said I will not, and Have you not, and He did not, and all the rest of it.

This passage presents one of Howells's few direct comments in his editorials about the language of romanticism. One of the main reasons he disliked romantic literature was the language, which he here labels as artificial. He uses Hawthorne as an example, which would imply that he did not care for Hawthorne. Actually, he greatly admired Hawthorne's fiction.

> But I believe we shall not always write the language in the present preposterous fashion, any more than we shall spell it as we now do; and that when we begin to write it as we speak it, we shall all be astonished and overjoyed, we who read as well as we who write, at its grace and ease.

This passage shows that Howells was obviously still not happy with the language of the literature of the day. He wanted it more "from the mouths of men." His desire that writers "write it as we speak it" was not a call for a "transcriptive" approach to literary language but simply a wish that writers would present speech and narrative as naturally as possible.

> In the meanwhile, I think that I can recognize in the use of dialect a tendency to the final freedom I hope for. The writer who has once used it, and felt his way through it to the life that language has on the lips of men, will never willingly abandon it; and I should not be altogether surprised if in the end he persuaded the general reader to bear with it. I can imagine the pleasure such a writer must feel in telling a whole story in dialect, in the person of some supposed narrator; but I do not think this pleasure can be greater, and I can see no reason why it should be greater, than that we should all have if we wrote the language naturally, or as we speak it.

As with most every other writer, Howells called for literary freedom of style and subject matter, but few other writers saw literary dialect as a vehicle for attaining such literary freedom.

> The use of dialect in modern literature is very modern, I think, and does not much antedate the present century. To be sure, Shakespeare makes his clowns talk like clowns, but their parlance is suggested, rather than represented, and after all there is very little of it.

This offers Howells's recognition that dialect had been used in the past, that the writers of his day and nation were not the first to use it. But he does contend that no group of writers had ever used it so accurately and effectively, or with the purpose of representing actual everyday speech faithfully.

As in the talk of Thomas Hardy's country folks, the personal rather than the provincial character of the speaker is suggested; and this is no doubt the ideal treatment of the vernacular in literature.

Howells liked Thomas Hardy, and here he identifies Hardy's effective use of dialect, an approach that Howells himself saw as an appropriate and fitting role of dialect in literature. Howells recognized the fact that Hardy did not use linguistic stereotypes but rather offered an idiolect for individual characters.

But if the writer feels that there is something of life which cannot be so imparted to the reader, he does well to represent the speaker's parlance more fully. Perhaps it was the cultivation of the Scottish dialect in poetry by Burns, and in prose by Scott, that gave the impulse toward writing dialect which has at least made the general reader tired. But this would not account for it in other languages and other lands, though there is no telling how quickly and intimately the different literatures influence one another.

Howells understands that literary dialect can easily be overused, and that the effects on the reader can be undesirable. He is ready to place the blame on the shoulders of Burns and Scott, despite the fact that their depiction of the Scottish dialect in their writing is considered a vital aspect of their literature and its popularity -- especially in Scotland.

The writer who seems to me above all others the master of the colloquial style in dialogue is Carlo Goldoni, who not only wrote entire comedies in dialect, but in his Italian comedies made his Venetians speak Venetian, with subtle distinctions between the accents of the city and of such a near-lying dependence as Chiogia. In Switzerland, the first great realist, Jeremias Gotthelf, as Pastor Bitzius called himself, wrote his novels of peasant life in the peasant dialect of the Canton of Berne; but as I know them only in the French translations, which, of course, do not reproduce the dialect, I am unable to judge of his fidelity in the work, though I have not the least doubt of it. In English fiction I have no very vivid impressions of dialect between Scott and Dickens, yet I know that Miss Edgeworth's Irish tales are full of it. Miss Austen, as far as I remember, eschews it altogether; and we must not, I suppose, call Fanny Burney's report of class vulgarisms dialect. No more can we class with dialect study the careful writing of thieves' slang which occupied the novelists of a much later day, and seems to have received even serious attention from Bulwer in his more youthful romances. When we come down to our own time, there is both the effect and the fact of dialect in George Eliot; but in Trollope there is not even the effect of it. There is a good deal of it in

Charles Reade, but I should be afraid that he got it up for the occasion rather than knew it from the lips of men; I have no proof of this, though. Mr. William Black suggests the Highland speech delightfully, but self-denyingly. Long before these writers the tribe of Irish novelists, represented by Lover and Lever, abounded in dialect, or at least brogue, and perhaps the Irish accent has been more heard in fiction than the negro, even; both are easy to do.

The vernacular of Dickens's people never seems to me quite trustworthy; he had not a good ear, and he had no scruple in perverting or inventing forms, if it suited his purpose. I fancy that his best and truest dialect writing is to be found in Hard Times, though he indulged in it everywhere in his novels. Thackeray's burlesque of the speech of serving men was always pure caricature; and Hardy appears to be the English novelist who reports the parlance of the common people with most liking and conscience. Wherever you come upon it in his books it is delightful; though, as I said, it is an imitation of their fashion of speech rather than a reproduction of it.

That final statement shows Howells's realization that literary dialect is and should be limited by practicality.

This is apparently the case with Giovanni Verga in his sketches of Sicilian life, and in his beautiful story of The House by the Medlar Tree. I do not think that the modern Italian writers have studied the provincial parlances at all in the degree that Goldoni did, and I know of very little Italian work in dialect among their later novelists. I am not saying there is none, but merely that I am ignorant.

In the Spanish novelists, whom I know a little better, I find a disposition towards it chiefly in Valdes, who amuses himself with the accents rather than the locutions of his Gallicians, and Andalasions, and Cubans, spelling them with great care, and imparting a sense both of personal and local character by means of them. If we come to the Germans, we have a whole dialect fiction created by Fritz Reuter in his Platt-Deutsch stories; but in French I cannot say how much has been done. In his earlier Books Zola gave us very abundantly of Parisian slang, but I suppose this was hardly writing dialect; and in his later books I do not remember any attempt to characterize his people by their peculiar speech. I have no sense of anything of the kind in Daudet, beyond a proverb or a phrase or two in Provencal, but I have not read Daudet so much in French, and I ought not to speak of him.

I have read only in English the great Russian writers, and I cannot even guess how much they have employed dialect. One can hardly imagine Tolstoy getting on without it, in books otherwise so faithful to the simple life they deal with. I read Norwegian no more than I read Russian, but my friend Professor Boyeson tells me that the Norwegian novelists and dramatists employ dialect a great deal, and that they employ it of set purpose, with the wish not only to portray the speech of the common people, but to give the strenuous and picturesque vocables and phrases of dialects permanent place in the written language. Ibsen, he says, studies the language of his characters so minutely that he suffers them to speak only and always as a man of this or that sort would speak, in the kind of personal vocabulary which we each have more or less to himself.

Again, Howells shows his breadth of reading material from around the world and his understanding of the subject by critiquing several authors based on their use of dialect in their works. This passage also illustrates his willingness to criticize or praise any writer -- no matter what his or her reputation may be -- based on his personal notions of literary language.

I do not know why I am saying all of this, unless to teach the general reader here that he is not the only general reader who has been obliged to bear with popular authors in the use of dialect. I should like to persuade him that our writers have not used it out of caprice, or merely to worry him, but have genuinely felt the need of it in their endeavors to portray a life new in so many of its phases to literature. Where this has been unconscious, it has been perhaps all the more genuine, for it has been part of the world movement in fiction towards greater naturalness and lifelikeness.

This is a simple plea aimed directly at the readers, a request that they understand why writers are using dialect in literature and that they show patience with it. He also offers his opinion that a writer's unconscious use of dialect is more effective, probably seeing it as being more natural. And it again shows Howells's acknowledgement of the negative aspects of dialect writing.

Without what has been done in this sort among us, I am sure we should not have the right we now undoubtedly have to a standing with the foremost of the peoples whose authors wished them to appear in literature exactly as they appear in life. I am always saying that it is not to any authors singly, or even very largely, that we are to look for the proof of this, but to the whole body of our authorship. We are an intensely decentralized people in our letters as well as in our politics, and the justification of dialect is to be found not in this quarter or that, but everywhere that our authors have honestly studied the local life.

Howells appeals to the reading public's sense of individualism and regionalism for justification of dialect in literature. He seems to want readers to claim ownership of the concept along with the writers.

> Lowell in Massachusetts and Riley in Indiana have been equally artistic in its employment, and there is no section or region without some writer emulous to report its life in the terms of its peculiar parlance, when they cannot be expressed without loss in the language common to all.

Again, Howells offers examples to support his observations. Here, he also contends that all parts of the country have writers willing and able to depict the "peculiar parlance" of their region.

> The general reader, however, has got tired of dialect, and the most conscientious artist must have moments when he would like to be friends with the mammon of unrighteousness. It will be well for him, perhaps, to consider how little dialect he can get on with, and how much can be done by suggestion, without actual representation. A great deal can be done, undoubtedly;

This passage shows Howells's realization that literary dialect need not be abundant. That realization is consistent with Sumner Ives's theories on the use of literary dialect (which are discussed in Chapter 5). Ives shows how compromise and incompleteness are necessary characteristics of effective literary dialect. This passage also shows that Howells's previous comment on wanting writers to "write it as we speak it" was not a call for writers to depict all the nuances, quirks, and characteristics of the dialects in their works. He realized that writers should not attempt to replicate actual spoken language.

> but when it comes to sacrificing a precious artistic effect, I should say that decidedly there could be no more question of the general reader's prejudices or sensibilities. In such a case, dialect must be used, and used unsparingly, and the author must trust to the recuperative forces of the general reader for a letter or final appreciation. Possibly, some aesthetic anaesthetic might be discovered which would paliate the worst immediate effects of the dialect, and carry the general reader through the chapters where it prevailed in a state of unconsciousness.

Howells reiterates his opinion that the importance of using dialect in literature surpassed the need for the reader to like the work. He again asks the reader to be patient and offers a tongue-in-cheek solution for the unpopularity of dialect. Presumably, if writers follow his earlier advice to rely more upon suggestion than representation of dialects, then no such "aesthetic anaesthetic" would be needed.

These passages illustrate two important points that are central to a study of Howells's attitudes towards literary language: (1) he felt literature -- all literature, not just that written in America -- should be written in a language that is alive and changing and real (the language of the common person); and (2) he often seemed to contradict that attitude both in his criticism and his fiction.

Howells's contradictory nature affected many aspects of his writing. Perhaps such contradictions were inevitable in light of his unwavering and intense calls for works that were thoroughly realistic in all respects. A man who demands total conformity to certain principles is asking for the impossible, even from himself, and Howells's career illustrates that. Even his own tendencies and preferences did not fall in line with what he espoused as desirable in literature. He called for writers to reflect the world around them in all its truth and reality, yet he shied away from the more gruesome and ugly aspects. He called for the language of literature to come from "the mouths of men," yet he drew the line at usage that was ungrammatical or crude. He was an innovator in literature, yet he wanted to uphold certain traditions and practices. He wanted to break the rules while also being the arbiter of good taste.

Numerous critics have recognized Howells's contradictory nature. The 1988 study by Elsa Nettels touches on this aspect of Howells often. She comments on Howells's desire to use literature as a unifying force to bring together the peoples of the country, yet he uses language to illustrate and exacerbate the differences and divisiveness. She also discusses his inconsistency in advocating and following his dictums for literary language:

> In identifying the forms of 'good natural English,' Howells proposed to break some of the grammarians' rules but insisted upon keeping others; he welcomed the new and the colloquial but condemned certain words and forms and cared to preserve certain distinctions. His guiding principle was that there should be one language, not two, that one should neither write what one would not say nor say what one would not write. . . . He imagined [this] writing, but did not write [it]. (25-26)

Nettels also writes of Howells's "'wicked pleasure' in knowingly violating rules upheld by arbiters like Lowell" (28), a pleasure one would not expect of Howells after reading some of his editorials (but would expect after reading others). Nettels also comments on Howells's conflicting tendencies towards the nature of literature:

> . . . Howells defined two tendencies in American literature: one toward "an elegance refined and polished, both in thought and phrase," the other toward "grotesqueness, wild and extravagant." Howells valued both strains and would not have sacrificed one for the other or have identified one as more "American" than the other. But clearly his contemporaries . . . placed Howells in the school of "the refined and polished," . . . . In particular, Lowell wished to claim Howells as his protege and disciple. Howells in turn wished to be so claimed but he also resisted the claim. He wished to be a guardian but he also wished to be a creator and an innovator. He would preserve decorum yet remain free to break rules. (39-40)

Why would a man who so ardently positioned himself at the forefront of the battle for realism in literature allow himself to be so contradictory? The reasons are complex and multiple.

Howells was a man of inconsistencies, a contradictory creature who seemed uncertain of his own tendencies, though he *thought* he was certain. Early in his career, Howells showed the makings of a romanticist; he evolved into a realist and then, in the waning years of his life, particularly after the deaths of his wife and of Mark Twain, his romantic sensibilities resurfaced. Such literary contradiction was combined with his professional dualities. He was an author and an editor/critic. Thus, he was the creator and the analyzer, the submitter and the acceptor. And as Nettels intimates, those complementary aspects of his being affected his attitudes about language. As a writer, he longed to break from the strictures of the language that had been established and protected by writers such as Lowell, but as a critic and editor of some of the most influential periodicals in the country, he felt a responsibility to maintain control of himself. In his years with *The Atlantic Monthly*, he not only reviewed works and evaluated them for acceptance or rejection, but he also was responsible for editing and correcting manuscripts through all stages of the publishing process. Thus, he was responsible for making sure the materials were correct and accurate; such responsibilities can reinforce a person's prescriptive tendencies. Had Howells been either a writer or an editor but not both, his approach to writing and his literary theories would probably have been more consistent (and most likely quite different).

What was there in Howells the man that made him such a study in contradictions? Was he simply a man given to change over the years, or was he a man at war with himself, constantly having to pit the preferences of his reason against those of his nature?

The search for answers to those questions can be found in Howells's youth. As a child, Howells showed signs of a mental precariousness. In childhood, he suffered from irrational fears, especially the fear of separation from his mother. As a young man, the primary obstacle to his leaving home and finding his way in the world was leaving his mother. For years, even after marrying and moving to Europe, he felt guilty at having left his mother. Perhaps this was, in part, due to his father. The senior Howells spent years moving his family from city to city, situation to situation, and Howells never really felt settled, geographically nor emotionally. Friendships were barely made before being abandoned. He felt secure only in his relationship with his mother. Her love was one of the few constants in Howells's life.

His father, a Swedenborgian and unmistakably the authority figure in Howells's life, was himself a man of contradictions. When Howells was young, his father tried to instill in him a sensitivity to those less fortunate than he and his family, and taught him to befriend all types of people. However, when Howells was thirteen, he became a companion to the dirtiest, "rag-tag" boy in the school. They played or fished every day after school. Despite this, they never became good friends, perhaps an early indication of Howells's tendency to act contrary to his feelings by responding to his father's teachings. The senior Howells did not like the boy and did not want his son spending time with him. So Howells ended the friendship. Such a basic contradiction between words and actions -- especially as seen in a parent by a child -- makes a lasting impression. The youth sees the possibility and utility of saying one thing and doing another.

Such events strengthened the ties between Howells and his mother but surely aggravated his mental condition. A child with little stability in friends, school, and family is certainly less likely to have inner stability. And so it was with Howells. In 1856, instability finally won; Howells suffered a mental breakdown and struggled with mental frailty the rest of his life.

Such experiences made it challenging for Howells to confront and write about the harsh, ugly realities of the world (though confront them he did, despite the contrary critical opinion). It is what prompted him, at one point in his career, to urge writers to concentrate on the "more smiling aspects of life." It is what compelled him to dislike the naturalists emerging in the last years of the 19th century, especially Stephen Crane, who Howells praised for his use of language but criticized for the earthiness of his subject matter. It is what tended to make him so inconsistent in his attitudes about his own profession.

CHAPTER 4

An Early Romantic

Within everyone lies the potentiality of every
character known to literature.
-- *Howells, 1894*

Growing up in the 1840's and coming of age early in the 1850's, Howells developed a natural love of the language and literature of the day. Those years were the heyday of America's first great writers --- James Fenimore Cooper, Ralph Waldo Emerson, Nathaniel Hawthorne, Washington Irving, Henry Wadsworth Longfellow, Herman Melville, Edgar Allan Poe, Henry David Thoreau, among others. So Howells's early impressions of great literature were shaped by the popular literature of the day -- romantic literature. What were the fundamental characteristics of the romanticism of the day? In 1785, Clara Reeve distinguished between the romance and the novel, and her distinctions summarize what were, for Howells, the distinctions between romanticism and realism:

> The Novel is a picture of real life and manners, and of the times in which it is written. The Romance in lofty and elevated language, describes what never happened nor is likely to happen --. The novel gives a familiar relation of such things as pass every day before our eyes, such as may happen to our friend, or to ourselves; and the perfection of it, is to represent every scene, in so easy and natural a manner, and to make them appear so probable, as to deceive us into a persuasion . . . that is all real, until we are affected by the joys and distresses, of the persons in the story, as if they were our own. (6)

Such a differentiation between the romance and the novel remained with Howells throughout his career -- through his romanticism and his realism. As we shall see later in this chapter, he labeled his first full-length fictional work a romance. And he called his third full-length work -- *A Foregone Conclusion* -- his first *novel.*

In essence, Howells saw Romantic works as depicting grand, heroic, unrealistic events and people being described with grandiose, flowery, and "unusable" language of such formality that no person would ever utter. He saw the use of such events, characters, and language as undesirable elements of fiction. Among his writings are numerous comments offering his opinions about romanticism:

> I know of none of [Goldoni's] plays that . . . insults common sense with the romantic pretense that wrong will be right if you will only paint it rose-color. (*Passions*, 210)

> . . . [T]here is always something fatally weak in the scheme of the pure romance, which, after the color of the contemporary mood dies out of it, leaves it in danger of tumbling into the dust of allegory . . . . (*Passions*, 187)

> . . . . [T]he romantic school does not count with me, for what is not true is not artistic. ("Favorite Novelist", 21)

That final comment summarizes Howells's prevailing attitude towards romanticism throughout the height of his career. However, he did not always hold this opinion towards romanticism. And he was never completely sold. He was an avid reader of Hawthorne and praised that author with many comments such as this: "I then preferred the region of pure romance where [Hawthorne] liked to place his action; but I did not find his instances the less veritable because they [were romantic]" (*Passions*, 186). He also wrote the following in *My Literary Passions:*

> But I have always had a great love for the absolutely unreal, the purely fanciful, in all the arts, as well as of the absolutely real; I like the one on a lower plane than the other, but it delights me, as a pantomime at the theatre does, or a comic opera, which has its being wholly outside the realm of probabilities. (216)

These do not sound like the opinions or reminiscences of a man completely devoted to realism.

Howells's childhood did not prepare him for a career of minimizing the importance of romanticism as a literary form. As a typesetter in various print shops owned by his father, he found himself at the hub of literary discussion in small-town Ohio. Through his interactions with literary-minded men, he heard frequent long-winded, critical discussions of America's writers and was introduced to writers from Europe. He was especially intrigued by the works of Heinrich Heine, a German whose career Howells's would mirror in that Heine was first entrenched in the romanticism of his country but was fighting to overcome those tendencies by developing his realistic perspectives. Heine espoused views that would eventually help to shape Howells's own realistic tenets.

But as many writers do, Howells started out by emulating the successful writers then in print. His earliest writings were tinged with romanticism. He began writing (and publishing) locally in his mid-teens. Early influences were Thomas Parnell and Donald Grant Mitchell (a.k.a. "Ik Marvel"). In *My Literary Passions*, Howells wrote of Parnell's "Battle of the Frogs and Mice":

> . . . it took me so much that I paid it the tribute of a bald imitation in a mock-heroic epic of a cat fight, . . . with the wonted invocation to the Muse, and the machinery of partisan gods and goddesses. (39)

Howells's "The Battle of the Cats" (1853) represents the youthful tendencies of imitative art, yet it also illustrates his interest at the time in such unrealistic "things" as Naiads, Nymphs, the Muses, and the "synods [of gods] on the summit of Olympus," including Saturn, Ulysses, Minerva, Narcissus, Lachesis, and Neptune. The opening lines illustrate the nature of this work:

> Again oh Muse, attune my listless lyre
> Celestial fervor let my song inspire
> Of warlike enemies once more I write,
> Who seek for vengeance in the chance of fight.
> Let Pallas, dreadful, with her hissing shield,
> And godlike wisdom guide th' ensanguined field;
> (quoted in Wortham, 10)

Yet that same year, he wrote "The Log Cabin," which he himself labeled a "beautiful sketch." Here readers can see an early example of the kind of writing that Howells is known for today. The opening paragraph immediately illustrates the simpler writing style and more realistic subject matter:

> By the side of a deserted highway, where the sound of your horse's hoof is broken by a thick growth of stunted grass, stands an old log cabin. It is one of those objects which sometimes meet your eye in the older parts of the country, and on which, for the sake of the past, you bestow a momentary thought. As you tie your horse to the gatepost, and tread the tangled pathway to the house, you pass the old well. Grass grows upon the curb, and almost hides it from you. The long sweep, with the grape vine rope, is broken in the middle, and lies athwart the curb, ... (quoted in Wortham, 19)

Howells's split tendencies towards the romantic and the real would characterize his early writing career. In 1854, he produced the following:

"A New Year's Glimpse of Memory Land"

> New Year's night, and the fire bright upon the hearth, and the old man alone in his room. It was ten o'clock by the city clock, which had just tongued the hour; ten by the clock on the mantelpiece; ten by the old man's watch.
>
> He was a strange, quiet person -- like a memory -- not a rosy, joyful memory -- but a dim, dark, shaded memory; a memory of something sorrowful; a relique of a woe. No one knew him, no one cared for the nasty old gentleman in black; yet he was a good, mild-looking man, not at all brusque or crabbed, but a little sad, may be. (quoted in Wortham, 22)

The first paragraph gives a straightforward, simple image of the setting, but the second paragraph shifts to a slightly different tone, a tone that presents a more romantic attitude or outlook, which can be seen (and felt) in wording that connotes mystery.

"A Sunny Day in Winter"

> The pools of water which the melted snow had made, stood glassily in the meadows, and the little swollen springs sparkled down the sides of the valley, like rich leaps of child-laughter, and lost themselves among the grass, or gurgled into the sedgy run that skirted the foot of the hill. A thin, warm mist rose from the stubble fields around, and clothed in its light vapor the base of the neighboring wood, whose top, rising bold and darkly at first, gradually melted away into the blue horizon beyond. The sky was serene and clear, and save two or three soft and lucid flakes that dozed

> upon its breast, was cloudless, while the sun looked down with summer smile. A quiet south wind stole soothingly along whispering among the leafless spray as softly as a blithe zephyr of June, and wafting now and then a snatch of a fragrance from the moist limbs of the maples and hickories. (quoted in Wortham, 26-7)

This passage presents a realistic subject matter that is tinged with a romantic tone, especially when Howells compares the wind to a "blithe zephyr."

"Dropped Dead: A Ghost Story"

> Years rolled on, as years will in time, and the old tavern was forsaken, and said to be haunted by Glen's ghost. Old ladies spoke of it in whispers, and the little boys, as they passed it after night, shut their eyes, and whistled. Nearly every one had a story to tell of the doings of the uneasy shade. Jones, the doctor, had seen a ball of fire hovering over Glen's grave in the burying ground, one damp, drizzly night. Grubbins, the blacksmith, as he was tottering home from a midnight wassail at the new tavern, was met by the sprite, who hurled him into a ditch, where the poor man's wife found him the next morning. By the elder folks he was sometimes seen washing his hands at the tavern pump, as he had done when he had first came into the village. (quoted in Wortham, 42-3)

The subjects of ghosts, along with words such as *wassail* and *sprite*, illustrate what Howells would later label as the most undesirable aspects of romantic fiction -- unreal subject matter and grand, uncommon words that were unfamiliar to much of the reading public.

"How I Lost a Wife: An Episode in the Life of a Bachelor"

> My friend Charley had any quantity of lovely sisters and cousins, to whom he introduced me, and with whom I fell in love -- *one* of whom, I should have said -- one of the sisters, Mary was her name. Sweet name! An angelic possessor of that sweet name! Could but those happy days be recalled -- could I but once more gaze into those brilliantly black eyes; could I but once more press to my palpitating heart that classic form; could I -- 'Hold your horses!' What am I talking about? I never got quite as far as this; suffice it to say, however, that I was 'up to my neck' in love with Mary, and I flattered myself she smiled approvingly on me. (quoted in Wortham, 46)

This is an interesting passage because Howells catches himself being overly romantic and puts on the brakes to return to a more accurate perspective and a more realistic description, based upon vernacular cliches rather than romanticized vocabulary.

"What I Saw at the Circus"

> And, as I saw all this, I forgot away some scores of years, and stood among the throng -- proud, and happy, and young. I was once more a devout believer in the verity of spangled dresses. The sallies of harlequino, were once more fraught with all their zest and freshness, and I felt an urchin's passionate longing for flesh-colored tights. I was once more filled with the determination that I felt so many years ago, to become proficient in the art of somersaulting; and had a vivid foreshadowing of my first appearance on the sawdust, as a ring-master.
>
> It was an idle revery, conjured up by an idle scene; and it was as well, perhaps, that I was abruptly roused from it by stumbling against a candyman's table. (quoted in Wortham, 56)

The opening paragraph above presents romanticized memories of a circus. The language is not characteristic of Howells's realism; it is not the language of the common man. The second paragraph shifts to a realistic tone.

These passages illustrate the mixed tendencies of Howells in his early writing. His subject matter showed more variety than in his later career during the strongest years of the realistic movement. In the works excerpted here, he has written a description of a winter day, a ghost story, a childhood recollection of a circus, the memories of a first love. And the language ranges from the simple style of the common man ("Grass grows upon the curb and almost hides it from you") to the more formal and less natural style of romantic literature ("The sallies of harlequino were once more fraught with . . . zest"). Thomas Wortham, editor of *The Early Prose Writings of William Dean Howells*, attempts to explain these mixed tendencies:

> Young Howells turned instinctively to his surroundings for literary material and attempted to find in them the meaning and commonday mystery that was for the romantic age to which he was heir the matter of the literary imagination. . . . [H]is attitude at the time toward his subjects was quite other from that dictated by the creed of literary realism that he would develop during the following decades. (26)

That last sentence refers to Howells's early attitudes towards his literary subjects. He saw romance all around him, and he embellished his observations and descriptions with a sentimentality and romanticism that were common characteristics of the popular literature of the day.

Howells's first extended work of fiction was published in serial form in the *Ashtabula Sentinel* in late 1854 and early 1855. "The Independent Candidate," an ambitious romance on the politics of the day, was a critical disaster. Forty years later, as he wrote *My Literary Passions*, Howells recalled the shame he felt over this incident, shame which still stirred bitterness even after four decades. He was tempted to try again to write on the same subject without the troublesome aspects of the romantic and sentimental, but he was still sufficiently upset about that episode of his life to be unable or unwilling to return to the topic.

Perhaps the main reason for the failure of this romance is that it brought together in one work both of Howells's tendencies – the romantic and the real. The subject is common and everyday -- small-town politics and the accompanying activities of a campaign. But the tone and supporting occurrences are inconsistent with the subject's realism. Love, insanity, amnesia, all colored with a tone of sentimental attachment -- these are used to loosely bring about the plot's climax and denouement. As Wortham notes, the story's "sentimental love interest and maudlin emotionality" coexist (and eventually triumph over) the "commonplace realities and situations, the humor and generally truthful portrayal of village life" (57). He also claims that, "had [Howells] kept his focus on the political issues and situations and shunned the sentimental and the romantic, he would have made something worth his time and tears" (57).

It is interesting to note, however, that in this early work Howells uses dialect to help develop character. The dialect here is reserved for the speech of a limited number of secondary, lower class characters. The character with the densest dialect features is John Trooze, a tavern landlord whose speech is heavily marked (affecting approximately 25% of the words) with non-standard features depicting mostly lexical and phonological variants, as illustrated in this passage:

> Now look here, oncet, . . . I've hearn tell walls has ears, an' ef walls hasn't, Sary Ann has. Sayin' she'd ha' happened to ben standin' at the door, there listenin' – as it's ony a wonder she wa'n't -- your cousin's cake 'ud ben dough in no time. (quoted in Wortham, 82)

The speech of two other characters -- Trooze's wife and Moro Gilky -- are also marked with dialect features (affecting approximately 10% of the words).

An interesting aspect of the dialect of these characters is that Howells did not regularly use literary dialect to represent the speech of his characters until many years later when he became more entrenched in the realist movement. In fact, as Nettels points out, Howells did not use dialect extensively until his twelfth novel, *The Minister's Charge,* which was published in 1887. The next chapter details the evolution in this aspect of Howells's literary methods.

Howells's pattern of part-time romantic/part-time realist continued through the late 1850's. In 1858, his bent seemed more towards the realistic. His story "Boots" presents an early use of colloquial language:

> There is not, as some stupid people have been led to think, a great deal of expression in the eye. The nose, however scrupulously followed by a second person, will not bring one acquainted with a man's character. The mouth, the brow, are often deceitful; and for those traitors that lurk under the hair of the head, what man . . . would have faith in them? How then, it is asked of me, is one to judge a man. Partly by letting him discover himself; chiefly by his boots. In them the whole mental man is glassed.
>
> I know very well that there are witty persons enough to say to this: But what if he wear gaiters? I am talking of men, not milk-sops. Only milk-sops wear gaiters. But women? Fie, sir! let the ladies' feet alone. (quoted in Wortham, 209)

Yet later in that same piece, Howells waxes romantic: "Strong minds impress this *ipsisimilitude* upon their weaker ones about them; and there is, under a wise Providence, force enough in every man to imbue his clothes with himself" (quoted in Wortham, 209).

That same year, a trip on a riverboat has him writing of his experiences in a way that foreshadows his future writing style. In a series of letters to his family, he describes the scenery and the passengers with such detail and accuracy that a reader can easily see his talents leading towards realism, especially *his* style of realism. Yet these observations are occasionally tinged with Romantic sentiment. As is Howells's pattern in many of his early writings, the following passage begins with a simple description of a common scene, but it then presents his emotional reaction to that scene, emotion that offers feelings of sentiment and longing, characteristics he later decried in literature as unrealistic (i.e. romantic):

> As we descend the river, the scenery, without lacking variety, becomes tamer and less picturesque. The hills are less frequent, the bottoms wider, and the banks lower. Yet, we passed some glorious scenery yesterday, which, to use a novel expression, cannot be appreciated unless seen. I was most enamored of a rustic mill that stood under a woody bluff, at the very river's brink, and with its overshot wheel and dashing stream that "Rolled a slumbrous sheet of foam below," looked the very picture of quietude and seclusion. It put me in mind of mills in sweet old German stories. (quoted in Wortham,106-7)

Later in 1858, Howells visited St. Louis via a riverboat ride on the Mississippi River. As with his earlier letters, the correspondence sent from this trip reflects a romantic vision but a realistic outlook. And he uses dialect to represent the speech of a fellow traveller, who commented on certain aspects of the trip being "so wery fillin' at the price" (quoted in Wortham, 115).

These letters of Howells's provide an interesting insight into the development of his craft as a writer and of his perspectives as a future critic. The writing style is simple and descriptive, and it focuses on common subjects. These letters provide what seems to be a more authentic voice for Howells in allowing him to simply concentrate on the reality that surrounded him on these trips. He did not need to concern himself with the elements of fiction, such as plot and character. Evidently, this made it easier for him to write naturally and simply. And these aspects were incorporated later into his theory of the language of literature -- prose was to be natural for the person writing it.

However, the romantic strain persisted in his fiction written at this time. His 1859 story "Geoffrey: A Study of American Life" seems to have come from the pages of Hawthorne or Poe:

> It was broad daylight when Geoffrey awoke. His dream was the merest vagary, and none but an idle man would have given it the thought with which he rose, and pondered upon that vision of his sleep. It was the sudden apparition of his cousin, whom he had loved. She seemed somehow to be breathed forth upon his perception in a tender light, that took her form and features and expression . . . . (quoted in Wortham, 254)

By 1860, when he was twenty-three, Howells had already put tens of thousands of words into the local newsprint. He had published romantic musings in his attempt to pay homage to his early favorites. He had also been faced with the need to describe actions, events, and people, and he knew he had to do so with an eye for accurate and faithful detail. The next logical step was to break into print with a more national audience. That year saw the production of *Poems of Two Friends*, a small volume that had half its pages devoted to verse from J.J. Piatt and the other half from Howells. Howells's verse, written during the latter 1850's, presents mostly his romantic side. He calls for the "Fisher-Maiden" to “Rest on my heart thy head, love/Nor tremble for fear of me” (128).

He offers "Words of Warning" that

> Wherefore, though the frown of heaven darken
> Love's blue sky,
> And thy soul in its forlornness hearken
> To thy darling's tremulous good-bye.
> Take thou heart, for all the world hath kindred
> To thy woe;
> Everywhere are longing spirits hindered
> By the cruel fate that bids thee go! (129)

Another poem "immortalizes" his thoughts on Sir Philip Sydney, "that most gentle knight,/In whom sweet love made shining deeds more bright" (132).

Howells's poetic efforts remind one more of Coleridge and Byron than of Whitman or Dickinson. They were blatantly imitative verse dictated by his admiration of Romantic poets rather than by his personal literary philosophy, which he had not yet formulated. As is commonly the case with young, impressionable minds, initial beliefs often mimic the beliefs of idols and heroes. And Howells idolized romantic writers.

In September 1861, just twenty-four years old, Howells was assigned to Venice as the American consulate, an appointment that was given to him in appreciation for the campaign biography he had written for Abraham Lincoln. Howells's years in Italy were to have a profound effect on his literary career. Upon his arrival, Howells was overcome with a severe case of homesickness, and he used his writing as a way to overcome his emotions. His early writings in Venice were true to what would become to him a vital aspect of literature -- he wrote about what he saw. But in those early years, he saw through romantic eyes. A man filled with nostalgia, home-sickness, longing for family and friends will naturally lean towards the sentimental in his writing (which is what Howells saw as the most glaring weakness of the romantic). Howells was no exception.

As he recorded his thoughts and impressions of Venetian life and as he depicted the people and the places, he did so in a style that, at times, was contrary to what he would later espouse, a style that also illustrated an inconsistency that would affect his writing through much of his career. Those early writings would later be transformed into Howells's first two book-length works -- *Venetian Life* (1866) and *Italian Journeys* (1867). Those works illustrate the transformation that was taking shape in Howells's literature.

Simply stated (perhaps too simply), Howells arrived in Venice a romantic and departed a realist, though at neither time was he wholly one or the other. As has already been illustrated in this chapter, Howells's early writings were more frequently than not romantic in their style and in their treatment of the subject matter. Early influence towards realism emanated from Howells's journalistic duties, which required him to "report" in a more straightforward, objective manner than he preferred. But his early Venetian writings illustrate his more romantic characteristics, perhaps understandably so in that the newness of the city's beauty and character exarcerbated Howells's romanticism. *Venetian Life*, published in 1866 but written during Howells's early years in Venice, illustrates his early romanticism. His commentaries on his Italian subjects concentrate more on his subjective responses to the people and the surroundings than on accurate description. This passage epitomizes the style throughout the work:

> The religious sentiment is deeply appealed to . . . in the interior of St. Mark's; but if its interior is heaven's, its exterior, like a good man's daily life, is earth's; and it is this winning loveliness of earth that first attracts you to it, and when you emerge from its portals, you enter upon spaces of such sunny length and breadth, set around with such exquisite architecture, that it makes you glad to be living in this world. . . .
>
> . . . The superb Imperial Palace -- the sculptured, arcaded, and pillared Procuratie -- the Byzantine magic and splendor of the church -- will it all be there when you come again to-morrow night? The unfathomable heaven above seems part of the place, for I think it is never so tenderly blue over any other spot of earth. (56-57)

Venetian Life is in excess of 400 pages, but this short passage is representative of the style (and attitude) throughout the book. Howells presents infatuation, love, sentimentality, and longing through the flowery "elevated" language that is more characteristic of his romantic predecessors than of his soon-to-be realistic contemporaries.

Italian Journeys was written during the later years of Howells's tenure in Venice and was published just one year after *Venetian Life*. But the writing style indicates a changed attitude toward Venice and toward his writing:

> There was little to interest us in the country over which we rode. It is perfectly flat, and I suppose the reader knows what quantities of hemp and flax are raised there. The land seems poorer than in Lombardy, and the farm-houses and peasants' cottages are small and mean, though the peasants themselves . . . looked well fed . . . . (45)

The perspective and the writing style differ in that, in this work, Howells begins with his realistic comments and remains with them, without wandering off into the romantic musings that had usually drawn his attention. Despite the Italian subject matter (which he truly was enamored with), he maintained more objectivity throughout this work.

What prompted Howells to turn towards such an overtly realistic attitude, and by extension, style? Of course, the realistic tendencies were fostered during his days as a journalist, and they accompanied him to Venice. But *Venetian Life* shows us that these journalistic tendencies were suppressed in the early days of his Venetian stay. What caused Howells's realistic tendencies to re-emerge?

Upon his arrival in Venice, Howells began to study the Italian language, which came to him easily and quickly, and he soon began reading Italian literature that had been inaccessible to him. This reading introduced him to the works of Carlo Goldoni, a Venetian playwright. Howells was struck with Goldoni's realism. He read Goldoni's autobiography in 1863 and immediately recognized what he believed was the true path for literature. Goldoni's work and the literary pronouncements in his autobiography seemed to awaken in Howells that dormant preference for realism that had been overshadowed by the romanticism he had developed in imitating the favorite writers of his youth.

In 1895, Howells published *My Literary Passions*, which was his look back at the literary models he admired and imitated, and from whom he learned. He writes of his reaction to Goldoni, whom he calls the "first of the realists" (208). Howells saw in Goldoni's work not only "truth in art" but truth that had *remained* truth in the Venice of Howells's day. As Howells writes of Goldoni's works,

> . . . [T]here is seldom anything more poignant in any of them than there is in the average course of things. The plays are light and amusing transcripts from life, for the most part, and where at times they deepen into powerful situations, or express strong emotions, they do so with persons so little different from the average of our acquaintance that we do not remember just who the persons are. (209)

He admired Goldoni's focus on ordinary things and ordinary people. Goldoni did not write of the grand and the beautiful and the magnificent in Italy. He focused on the real, and Howells took note and was profoundly affected.

Howells goes on to recall that none of Goldoni's plays "insult[ed] common sense with the romantic pretense that wrong will be right if you will only paint it rose-color" (210). Essentially, what Goldoni gave Howells was the realization that literature could be truthful *and* beautiful *and* real *and* universal. This realization is what helped Howells develop the beginnings of what would grow to be his theory of realism in literature. Goldoni also helped Howells realize that the commonplace and the probable could be as beautiful and as meaningful as the romantic.

Howells also remembered another effect Goldoni had on him: "[H]e had the power of taking me out of my life, and putting me into the lives of others, whom I felt to be human beings as much as myself" (211). The effects that Howells felt from this Venetian playwright would be enormous and historical, for those Italian plays helped to shape what would become quite influential attitudes within Howells. As Van Wyck Brooks explains, "Howells [saw] that if he was going to do anything worth while, he would have to get into fiction from life the things that had not been got into fiction before . . . ." (*Coming of Age*, vii). This realization would help to shape the literature of America for decades to come, although it did not reshape Howells's own prose immediately.

When Howells returned from Italy, he wrote of Venice in *Venetian Life* and *Italian Journeys*, which were followed by *No Love Lost* (1869) and *Suburban Sketches* (1871). *No Love Lost* is subtitled "A Romance of Travel," which indicates the author's intentions and the nature of the work. *Suburban Sketches*, despite a title that seems to suggest realistic writing, presents an inconsistent combination of romanticism and realism. On the first page, Howells writes of a "storm of snow and rain so finely blent by the influences of this fortunate climate, that no flake knew itself from its sister drop . . . " (11). He continued a few lines later:

> A vernal gale from the east fanned our cheeks and pierced our marrow and chilled our blood, while the raw, cold green of the adventurous grass on the borders of the sopping sidewalks gave, as it peered through its veil of melting snow and freezing rain, a peculiar cheerfulness to the landscape. (11)

However, a few pages later, Howells's prose becomes noticeably more realistic:

> . . . these orphans do not seem to grieve much for their bereavement, but lead a life of joyous and rather indolent oblivion in their quarter of the city. They are often to be seen sauntering up and down the street by which the Charlesbridge cars arrive, -- the young with a harmless swagger, and the old with the generic limp which our Autocrat has already noted as attending advanced years in their race. (18)

The first passage again has the feel of the sentimentality, subjectivity, and overstatement of Howells's earlier Romantic works. But the second passage becomes more objective, more straightforward in its perspective and its feeling.

In these sketches, Howells also attempts to depict dialect consistently in the speech of one of his characters for the first time since "The Independent Candidate." (The following chapter will discuss literary dialect in more detail.) *Suburban Sketches* seems to represent a bridge between the romanticism of Howells's early career and the realism of his future career.

But there is disagreement among the critics as to when Howells the Romantic was fully transformed into Howells the Realist. Olov Fryckstedt summarizes the varying opinions:

> Different periods have been suggested as the most likely time when Howells ceased to be a romantic poet and became a realistic prose writer. Parrington assumes that Howells was a realist by instinct and never approved of romanticism; Walter Blair and James Woodress point to the Venetian dramatist Goldoni, . . . as the decisive influence; Cornelia Kelly suggests that Howells' friendship with James in the middle sixties made him break with romanticism and adopt realism. Everett Carter attributes great significance to Howells' acquaintance with Hippolyte Taine's literary theories in the early seventies. Robert Falk does not think that we can safely call Howells a realist until the early eighties. (64)

An Early Romantic

This chapter and those that follow illustrate aspects of Howells's fiction that indicate that his conversion to realism cannot be pinpointed exactly and also that it was never complete. His romantic sensibilities dominated his writing during his early career but gave way to his realistic tendencies as his career developed. But those romantic sensibilities never left him completely. In the introduction to the University of Indiana's edition of *Their Wedding Journey*, John K. Reeves discusses Howells's internal warring of literary principles, labeling it the author's "head-heart conflict":

> The question of whether Howells had left the romantic poet behind on the road to becoming a realist is more complex because it involves a conflict within him of which he was only partly aware. Intellectually, he had been dedicated, from at least the time of "Geoffrey Winter," to the principle of telling the truth about life, but his emotional nature often made him see this "truth" in conventional romantic hues. (xxv)

As early as 1924, Oscar Firkins had this to say about Howells's internal battle between romanticism and realism:

> I am sometimes doubtful whether romanticism proper is the true object of Mr. Howells's antipathy. He abhors stale tricks; he detests the morbid in morality and immorality alike. These things are not infrequent in romance, but it is not clear that they constitute its essence, or that to its essence he is inherently hostile. (279)

As Howells's career as a novelist began to take shape in the early 1870's, as he put more and more words on paper, his realistic principles (the principles for which he is well known) slowly began to dominate his writing and his criticism.

CHAPTER 5

Literary Dialect and the Path to Realism

. . . nothing more and nothing less than the
truthful treatment of materials.
Howells, 1891

In 1872, Howells published *Their Wedding Journey*, clearly with the intentions of offering a more realistic depiction of the world around him. How successful Howells was in achieving this purpose has been a subject of debate. Is this work Howells's finest novel, as Theodore Dreiser claimed? Is it a "faithful and pleasing picture of our American existence," as Henry Adams described it? Or is it a step towards realism with the back foot still firmly planted on the doorstep of romanticism?

With *Their Wedding Journey*, Howells was consciously taking a step down what he described as "a path in literature which no one else has tried, and which I can make most distinctly and entirely my own" (xiii). This path may have become illuminated to him as he assumed more editorial duties at the *Atlantic*, which included the reviewing of current American and European fiction. In a January 1870 review of Thomas Bailey Aldrich's *The Story of a Bad Boy*, Howells wrote, "There must be a great deal of fact mixed up with the feigning, but the author has the art which imbues all with the same quality, . . ." (*Atlantic Monthly*, January 1870, 124). Aldrich's work undoubtedly had an impact on Howells's literary attitude, for not long after that review appeared, Howells started writing *Their Wedding Journey*.

And his starting point for this work was his own travel diary written during the trip he and his wife took earlier that same year.

Their Wedding Journey was a step toward realism, but it was just a step. This book "offers a unique opportunity to see Howells the journalist, romantic poet, and travel essayist taking early steps towards becoming Howells the realistic novelist" (*TWJ*, xxii). In fact, John K. Reeves, editor of the University of Indiana's edition of *Their Wedding Journey*, claims that a study of Howells's manuscript shows signs that he revised with the specific intention of eliminating "romantic attitudes and responses" (*TWJ*, xxv). But Reeves also states that several of Howells's revisions "suggest that [he] toned down his realism to suit his genteel audience" (*TWJ*, 220). Such a duality in his approach is certainly consistent with the inconsistencies discussed earlier.

This work introduces Basil and Isabel March, a couple modeled loosely upon Howells and his wife. The Marches are important characters in an analysis of Howells's literary development because they appear in eight works, from *Their Wedding Journey* in 1872 to *Their Silver Wedding Journey* in 1899. Thus, their depiction, their attitudes, and their language -- as well as those of the characters around them -- reflect Howells's development as a realist.

A focused analysis of Howells's literary dialect, based on the principles set forth by Sumner Ives in his seminal treatment, "A Theory of Literary Dialect," elucidates and illustrates the path of Howells's realism. Ives's work, which first appeared in 1950, was intended as an extension and revision of the work done on literary dialect by George Phillip Krapp in the 1920's. Ives recognized (as did Howells) that literary dialect is a legitimate and important tool for writers in their attempts to establish realistic fiction. He contends that dialect writers (most of them, anyway) intend to depict dialects accurately, though their depictions are deliberately incomplete.

Ives offers several central premises related to how writers use dialect in their fiction:

* Dialect characters are distanced -- socially or geographically – from the other characters in the work.
* The differences suggested by dialect often connote inferiority.
* Writers do not usually attempt to depict dialects as they are spoken. Rather, they will identify a small number of easily identifiable and characterizable features that will readily help to characterize speakers of the dialect.

* Since few writers are linguists, their depictions tend to be inaccurate and inconsistent, with the attempts at written representation being, at times, ineffective and unclear.
* Writers tend to treat their own regional and social concepts of standard English as the norm, and they depict as non-standard any feature that deviates from that concept of norm.
* In the interest of making their characters recognizable and their fiction readable, writers tend to regularize dialects more than actual speech warrants.

This final point is important in Ives's overall theory. As he states:

> When an author uses a dialect as a literary medium, or represents any of his characters as speaking dialect, it is [a] typical set of usages . . . that he employs. . . . [J]ust as the author constructs the characters themselves from his experience with many persons, gathering traits from many individuals, so he develops his dialect from his observations of many persons speaking it. From the total linguistic material available, he selects those features that seem to be typical, to be most representative of the sort of person he is portraying. These features he generalizes so that the literary dialect is likely to be more regular in its variants than the actual speech it represents. (153)

Ives also identifies the methods writers used to depict those features:

> [p]ronunciation features . . . suggested by systematic variations from the conventional orthography, or "phonetic" re-spelling; grammatical forms . . . that do not appear in the textbooks -- except as awful warnings; and words . . . that are not commonly found in abridged dictionaries. (147)

Ives's primary thesis is that writers of dialect use a relatively small number of regular dialect markers to indicate features that are nonstandard in their own dialects to characterize speakers in their fiction.

In general, the language of Basil and Isabel March changes little throughout their appearances in Howells's works. As will be illustrated in more detail, the Marches' speech is relatively unmarked. That fact is consistent with Ives's theory that authors who depict dialect through non-standard spelling, vocabulary, and syntax will use their own concepts of acceptability as the basis for the unmarked dialect, because "[l]acking a uniform standard for spoken English, the author has no choice but to use the accepted criteria for his own region" (Ives, 158). Ives observes further that "authors see little reason to write as dialect what is to them good English" (165).

Despite the fact that Howells was an ardent proponent of realism in all aspects of literature, including language, he also was a prescriptivist when it came to the rules and usage of English, an inconsistency discussed earlier. Thus, it is no surprise that characters based on himself and his wife, characters who appear more frequently in his fiction than any other characters, would use speech that is marked with few dialect features. And interestingly, the dialects of both Basil and Isabel March were similar in the density of their dialect markers, an indication of Howells's attitudes towards his own wife and her equality with him.

Even as Howells's devotion to realism grew, the language of the Marches showed no increase in the number of dialect features. A close study of representative passages from five of the works in which the Marches appear shows that the density of dialect features is extremely low and consistent, ranging from .36% of the words in their dialogue to just over 1%. (In this study, the term *dialect marker* is used to refer to any feature that is marked as being different from formal, standard speech. This study is not concerned with identifying and analyzing the nature of Howells's various usages; that is, with whether they are examples of differing dialects, colloquialisms, or registers. The primary focus here is with Howells's overall representation of speech and how he chose to mark it as being different from his personal concept of standard English.)

The methodology used in this analysis is based on the approach described by Alvin Gregg in two papers he delivered in 1983 on the literary dialect in the works of William Faulkner. Gregg calculated the density of dialect markers as percentages by counting the number of words in a character's dialogue and then counting how many of those words are marked with some type of dialect feature. As he admits, such percentages can sometimes be misleading in that some words can reflect more than one dialect feature, such as the spelling of "wasn't" as "wuzn'," which includes both eye-dialect spelling and the deletion of the final consonantal phoneme. However, since the percentages here are being used to illustrate a pattern in Howells's works, rather than the exact markers used, such slight inaccuracies are insignificant.

As with Gregg's method, representative passages of dialogue were selected; then, the number of words spoken by each character were counted, and the number of those words that were marked with some feature that indicated it as being non-standard were counted. (A more detailed example of how this analysis was calculated is illustrated in the appendix.) The study focused on both Basil and Isabel March, as well as other characters that appear in the same works. The five works selected for this study were:

Their Wedding Journey [TWJ]	1872
"Niagra Revisited" [NR]	1883
A Hazard of New Fortunes [HNF]	1889
"A Pair of Patient Lovers" [PPL]	1897
Their Silver Wedding Journey [TSWJ]	1899

The following chart provides the results of the analysis of the speech of the Marches in those five works:

Work	# Words Analyzed	# Markers	Percentage
TWJ	2188	22	1.0
NR	1624	13	.8
HNF	7926	70	.88
PPL	3870	14	.36
TSWJ	1507	16	1.06

Of the 135 dialect markers identified, the majority of them (102, or approximately 75%) represent lexical items, while only four markers (or approximately 3%) present phonological variations. These numbers are consistent with Howells's personal tendencies towards realism and acceptable usage in his own speech. Of the various types of dialect features, lexical items are often less socially stigmatized than are variants in grammar, syntax, or pronunciation. Whereas differences in vocabulary are often labeled as interesting or quaint, differences in grammar, syntax, and pronunciation are more likely to be considered awkward or nonstandard, although regional variations in pronunciation are more readily accepted than are variations in syntax and grammar.

Even though the density of dialect features was consistent for the Marches throughout their frequent appearances in Howells's fiction, their language did not remain the same. The style of their speech did change, reflecting Howells's growing commitment to realism. Accompanying these changes in the Marches' language (which are illustrated in the succeeding sections) was a change in the number of dialect markers in the language of the characters surrounding the Marches in the works studied. As Howells's realism became a stronger characteristic of his writing, the incidence of dialect marking increased. These two changes -- in the speech style of the Marches and in the dialect of the other characters -- will be analyzed for each of the five works.

Their Wedding Journey : Introducing the Marches

Basil and Isabel March make their initial appearance in Howells's first full-length work of fiction, *Their Wedding Journey*. Howells saw this work as representing something new in literature. It focuses on the wedding trip of a newlywed couple. The action is minimal. The novel presents this couple's reactions to the people and places around them, and those reactions are colored with a romanticism that seems natural from a young couple on their honeymoon.

Consider Basil's commentary on the joy of being newly married, which contains sentimental overstatement, an aspect of the language of romanticism that Howells later disliked:

> I always knew that I was not a very handsome or other-wise captivating person, but I can remember years – now blessedly remote -- when I never could see a young girl without hoping she would mistake me for something of that sort. . . . I dare say all young men are so. . . . Blessed be marriage, I am free at last! All the loveliness that exists outside of you, dearest -- and it's mighty little -- is mere pageant to me; . . . . (48-49)

The final three lines epitomize the romantic sentimental hyperbole in this passage.

Isabel's subsequent description of a past meal is also similarly tinged with the hyperbole of romanticism:

> I remember the freshness and brightness of everything on the table, ... They seemed to have been preparing that breakfast for us from the beginning of time, and we were hardly seated before they served us

with great cups of *cafe'-au-lait*, and the sweetest rolls and butter; then a delicate cutlet, with an unspeakable gravy, and potatoes -- such potatoes! (60)

The young newlyweds -- a romantic and standard-English-speaking couple in Howells's eyes -- encounter dozens of people during their travels, but few of them have speech marked by dialect features. Those who do have a dialect are blue-collar or ethnic characters who appear only briefly. Just as noticeable are the instances when it seems that some sort of dialect markers would have been appropriate and effective but did not appear. The following excerpts identify the dialect characters. The words or phrases that are marked with a dialect feature are underlined:

A Hebrew businessmen encountered on a touring boat:

Well, as I was a-say'n', Isaac don't seem to haf no natcheral pent for the glothing business. Man gomes in and wands a goat, . . . Isaac'll zell him the goat he wands him to puy, and he'll make him believe it's the goat he was a-lookin' for. . . . A man gan't zugzeed that goes upon that brincible. (50)

A "conventional American hotel clerk" in Rochester, NY:

Well, she's a mighty pooty gul, any way, Chawley! (70)

A traveler from New York encountered by Basil on the boat whose speech he inconsistently reports to Isabel in that the first line contains dialect markers, whereas the second statement does not:

He said, "Pretty tejious waitin', ain't it?" in the best New York State accent."
. . . "O," says he, " I'm glad you like it, and it's not the least offence to ask. . . ." (126)

A carriage driver in Montreal:

I had a party from the States, ma'am, yesterday, . . .two ladies, real heavy ones, two gentlemen, weighin' two hundred apiece, and a stout young man on the box with me. You'd 'a' thought the horse was drawin' an empty carriage, the way she darted along. (137)

A female encountered in Quebec:

> Of course, if I'd known 'ow it really was, I never would 'ave listened to such a thing, never. And there isn't another 'ole in the 'ouse to lay me 'ead. (177)

A "troupe of British blondes . . . appearing in Quebec":

> "W'at, -- w'at are we going to give at Montrehal?"
> "We're going to give 'Pygmalion', at Montrehal."
> "But we cahn't, you know . . .; Hagnes is gone to New York and there's nobody to do Wenus."
> "Yes, you know, . . . oo's to do Wenus?"
> "Bella's to do Wenus."
> ". . . 'Ow ever would she get herself up for Wenus? . . .W'at a guy she'll look! . . . Nonsense! Bella's too 'eavy for Wenus. . . . Charley don't seem so well this afternoon. . . . Poor Charley, let's go and cheer 'im hup a bit." (160-61)

These excerpts show that, even though Howells did not depict a large number of dialect features in any passage, he used many different types of features, such as phoneme deletion ("pooty gul" for "pretty girl""), phoneme insertion ("Montrehal"), variant pronunciation ("tejious" for *tedious*, "cahn't" for *can't*), subject/verb disagreement ("Charley don't seem"), and eye-dialect spellings ("natcheral").

As noticeable as the dialect characters in this work are, there are instances when literary dialect would seem to have been appropriate, yet none is depicted:

In an emergency situation on a boat when several passengers are shouting orders or cries for help:

> 'Send out a boat!' 'There was a woman aboard that steamboat!'
> 'Lower your boats!' 'Run a craft right down, with your big boat!'
> 'Send out a boat and pick up the crew!' (53)

These statements are even punctuated as exclamations, yet the language is depicted as standard and unmarked.

French nuns who are said to be speaking English with a French accent, but no accent is depicted:

> Breathe it, . . . sometimes the air of the hospital offends. Not us, no; we are used; but you come from the outside. It is very little to see, . . .; but if you are pleased, I am very glad. Good by, good by! (159)

The Marches' first appearance is touched by romance and romanticism, as Howells's first full-length work of fiction has not yet taken him completely away from the style of his early idols. He has the Marches speaking with the flowery style of hyperbole and sentimentality he associated with romanticism. Their language shows no signs of being anything but standard English. It contains no variations in pronunciation, grammar, or lexicon that would appear to be dialectal. And Howells represented only a limited number of dialect features in the speech of a few of the characters the Marches encounter on their journey.

"Niagra Revisited": The Marches Twelve Years Later

This story visits the Marches on another trip. Nearly a dozen years of marriage have, predictably, had an effect on Basil and Isabel. They not only have a family now, but they also have an altered perception of marriage, as described in a passage about Isabel:

> Marriage was not the poetic dream of a perfect union that a girl imagines it; she herself had found that out. It was a state of trial, of probation; it was an ordeal, not an ecstasy. (*TWJ*, 207)

This altered perception is reinforced in the changed speech of the husband and wife, whose dialogue with one another is less romantic than it was eleven years earlier. On this trip, they are taking their children to Niagra, which they had visited during their wedding journey. This combination of a romantic idea -- revisiting a place with youthful, romantic associations -- and symbols of life's real existence -- children -- is illustrated in the inconsistencies of the speech of Basil and Isabel. In fact, Isabel voices concern at their having come, afraid that the whole trip will destroy the youthful and romantic perspective they had gained of the place during their honeymoon. Basil is less concerned, though not too certain.

These inconsistencies and changes in perspectives and attitudes are reflected in their language. Their language retains its romantic aspects of hyperbole and sentimentality when listeners are present. Underlined passages illustrate this romanticism.

> *Basil* : Yes, . . . it is our own Enchanted City. I wonder if that unstinted hospitality is still dispensed by the good head waiter at the hotel where we stopped, to bridal parties who have passed the ordeal of the haughty hotel clerk. I wonder what has become of that hotel clerk. Has he fallen, through pride, to some lower level, or has he bowed his arrogant spirit to the demands of advancing civilization, and realized that he is the servant, and not the master, of the public?
> *Isabel* : All that is sacred to those dear young days of ours; and I wouldn't think of trying to repeat it. Our own ghosts would rise up in that dining-room to reproach us for our intrusion! O, perhaps we have done a wicked thing in coming this journey. We ought to have let the past alone; we shall only mar our memories of all these beautiful places. (*TWJ*, 193-94)

But when Basil and Isabel are alone, their comments to each other become simpler, more straightforward, less romantic. The passages I have underlined reflect a more common, realistic, down-to-earth attitude towards the world and the people around them, as well as their feelings and perceptions of each other.

> Basil, . . . it would be disgusting! I wouldn't do it for the world -- not even for *that* world. I saw one middle-aged couple . . . sitting on some steps, he a step below her, and he seemed to want to put his head on her knee; but I gazed at him sternly, and he didn't dare. We should look like them, if we yielded to any outburst of affection. Don't you think we should look like them? I don't know, ... You are certainly a little wrinkled, my dear. And you are very fat, Basil. We couldn't look young if we quarreled a week, . . . We better content ourselves with feeling young, ... (*TWJ*, 204-5)

Despite these changes in their outlook and their language, Howells uses few distinctive dialect features in representing the speech of Basil and Isabel. As was the case with their previous trip eleven years earlier, they encountered few speakers whose speech was marked with dialect. In fact, the only marked dialect speech in this story (other than a few lexical items from the Marches) belongs to a driver, just one line representing an informal style: "You can come back and see 'em on your bridal tower" (201).

This short story is more or less an extension of *Their Wedding Journey*, with slight alterations in the outlook of a husband and wife who have now been married eleven years. But those alterations have a significant effect on the characters and on their speech.

A Hazard of New Fortunes: The Marches in the "Real" World

By the mid- to late '80's, Howells's fiction was changing. As he became a more ardent advocate of realism and more committed to writing of the common and the low, his works became more realistic in their plots, characters, and language. Howells came to rely increasingly on dialogue and dialect to characterize the people of his novels. The primary example of this approach appeared in 1889, which also happens to be the next appearance of Basil and Isabel March.

A Hazard of New Fortunes is one of Howells's most critically acclaimed novels and represents a transition in Howells's literature. It is the first novel he wrote after moving to New York. It is his most social novel. And not coincidentally, it also includes more representation of dialect than do any of his other novels.

In the bibliographical note prefacing the novel, Howells explains his reasons for bringing Basil and Isabel back and the changes that were necessary for them to be in this work:

> In venturing out of my adoptive New England, . . . I found it natural to ask the company of these familiar acquaintances, but their company was not to be had at once for the asking. When I began speaking of them as Basil and Isabel, in the fashion of *Their Wedding Journey*, they would not respond with the effect of early middle age which I desired in them. They remained wilfully [sic], not to say woodenly, the young bridal pair of that romance, without the promise of novel functioning. It was not till I tried addressing them as March and Mrs. March that they stirred under my hand with fresh impulse, and set about the work assigned them as people in something more than their second youth. (3)

Accompanying this change in role and purpose for the Marches was a further simplification of their language. Their speech is much less flowery and romantic than it was when they first appeared on their wedding journey; it is simple, common, everyday. However, it remains relatively unmarked dialectally and comparatively standard when cast beside the language of the other characters in the novel.

The Marches' speech contains more dialect markers in this work than in any other, but since they have a great deal more dialogue, the density of the dialect features remains about the same as in the previous works. Nonetheless, the Marches' speech is noticeably different in tone. The following words and phrases -- which are examples of informal idioms and usages -- appear in their language:

stands to reason	oughtn't
putting the best foot forward	whip-hand
if the worst come to worst	live in the spirit
not the half of it	winks out
bare bones	to lay up
to blink them	pshaw
at a pinch	on the spot
take it out of me	stick to it
made way with ourselves	run your chance
a good many	to take hold

These examples illustrate Howells's depiction of a more natural style, a more realistic dialogue (though still relatively unmarked). In earlier works, the Marches' speech contained no such idiomatic usages. They are the product of the changes in Howells's perspectives on life and literature.

But even more telling of those changes is the speech of the characters that surround the Marches in this novel. In earlier works, the Marches do encounter dialect speakers during their travels, but as has already been illustrated, those dialects are few and far between, and they belong to lower class, ethnic characters. Most characters are given standard speech.

But in *A Hazard of New Fortunes*, for the first time in Howells's fiction, the primary dialect characters are also the primary characters in the novel, with central roles in the plot. They include Berthold Lindau, the Woodburn family, and the Dryfoos family. Two other primary characters -- Fulkerson and Angus Beaton -- have significantly less dialect.

Berthold Lindau

Berthold Lindau is an elderly German refugee who is an old friend of Basil March's from the West. His English is clearly marked with a German accent, which is not surprising until one recalls that, in *Their Wedding Journey*, the Marches encountered French nuns speaking English with a French accent that Howells chose not to depict in his representation of their speech.

An analysis of representative passages of Lindau's dialogue shows a density of dialect markers of approximately 28%; that is, more than one quarter of his words contain some type of dialect marker. Of 614 words of dialogue examined, 172 were marked with a dialect feature. Since these markers are Howells's attempt at portraying a German accent, nearly all the markers are phonologically based, although some are grammatically based, such as the omission of articles. The markers are widely varied and, at times, inconsistently used. The vast majority involve consonantal sounds. The most common markers include these:

orthographical:	"d" or "t" > "dt"	61	35.46%
phonological:	[k] > [g]	25	14.62%
	[b] > [p]	17	9.88%
	[s] > [z]	12	7.00%
	[v] > [f]	9	5.23%

The representation of Lindau's German accent seems, at times, too dense in its markers, to the point of affecting the readability of Lindau's speech. But Howells's representation of this accent is consistent with Ives's contention that, in an attempt to regularize dialect, authors may exaggerate certain features. Howells has done that with Lindau, though it must be remembered that his speech represents a different type of dialect than appears in the speech of other characters. Lindau's speech is marked by the phonological features of another language, his native language. Thus, the "intruding" phonological features would naturally occur more often.

In a few places, Howells allows a few inconsistencies to slip through. For example, in one place he has Lindau say "dell me," while a few pages later, Lindau says "tell me." Another example involves the word *young*, written alternately "yong" and "yo'ng". That alternation seems to be a purely typographical inconsistency. By contrast, the alternation between *dell* and *tell* may be due to an oversight by Howells, or it may reflect his recognition that dialect variants occur inconsistently in speech, as Ives points out. Similar examples of sound pairs that seem to alternate in free variation include the following:

see > zee	has > hass
twenty > tventy	village > willage
tell > dell	dear > tear
cheaper > jeaper	just > chust
boy > poy	poet > boet
gay > cay	country > gountry

Again, these variations may be oversights, or they may be accurate representations of the idiolect of a non-native speaker of English. As Ives reminds us, novelists are not linguists, and though Howells comes closer than most writers to being a combination of the two, his primary objective in his literary dialect is characterization, not linguistic accuracy.

Another interesting aspect of Lindau's speech to note is that, in the few instances he is described as speaking German, his language is represented in standard English. All dialect markers disappear from his language. In other words, Howells is denoting that Lindau is speaking an unmarked, standard version of his native language, which must be presented in English so his readers can understand it.

The Dryfoos Family

Jacob Dryfoos is a former Ohio farmer, a rather crude, elderly capitalist who is the financial backer of a publishing venture. His wife, Elizabeth, is a backwoods country woman, with whom he has three children. Whereas the dialects of Basil and Isabel March (and their children, in later works) are close to identical in their density of features, the dialects of Jacob Dryfoos and his children differ noticeably from the language of Elizabeth. The speech of Jacob and the children has a very low density of markers -- approximately 5%. The dialect markers in their language consist primarily of these features:

eye dialect spellings (e.g. "staid" for *stayed*)
use of *ain't*
omission of letters denoting sound changes or deletion (*goin'*, *'em*)
nonstandard verb forms ("He done it")
nonstandard pronoun case ("us girls, we brazened it")
lexical items (*middlin', nohow, reckon)*

These characters, despite their rural Midwest background, speak a relatively unmarked dialect. However, Elizabeth's speech has nearly triple the incidence of features, at approximately 14%. The types of features included in her speech also highlight its nonstandard aspects. Elizabeth's dialect contains all the features identified above plus a few more types (such as double negatives), as well as a much higher density of dialect features. The following passage is representative (with underlining indicating those words marked with a dialect feature):

> You <u>hain't</u> never <u>heared</u> <u>o'</u> the Dunkards, I <u>reckon</u>, . . . Some <u>folks</u> <u>calls</u> <u>'em</u> the <u>Beardy</u> Men, because they <u>don't never</u> shave; and they wash feet like they do in the Testament. My uncle was one. He raised me. (157)

Compare that with the following passage spoken by Jacob:

> Here, take my handkerchief. I've got a nice lot in the cemetery, and I'm <u>goin'</u> to have a monument, with two lambs on it -- like the one you always liked so much. It <u>ain't</u> the fashion, any more, to have family <u>buryin'</u>-grounds; they're <u>collectin'</u> <u>'em</u> into the cemeteries, <u>all round</u>. (228)

What might have been Howells's reasons for giving the mother a more marked dialect than those of the rest of her family? One might conjecture that Howells identified with Jacob, who was a displaced Midwesterner in New York City interested in the publishing game. The children were young, idealistic, not socially astute but social-minded nonetheless. By contrast, the mother was neither socially nor professionally ambitious, and such a lack of concern in these areas could result in less concern with her language, as well.

Howells's depiction of more dialect in the speech of the older woman of the family may be more accurate than it at first seems. Dialectologist Walt Wolfram has studied the speech differences between the genders, and one of his conclusions is that "it is not uncommon to find older women to be more conservative than men in retaining some of the relic forms of the regional dialects" (123). One might also conjecture that the male dialect was more subject to change since men were more frequently in conversation with speakers of different dialects.

<u>The Woodburns</u>

Colonel Woodburn is a Southerner from Virginia who has come to New York for business purposes. He is accompanied by his daughter, Madison. The dialogue of both father and daughter are given phonological features indicating a Southern accent, though the daughter's speech is more densely marked. The density of dialect features in her speech is approximately 28%, while the Colonel's dialect has a density just under 7%. Their speech is marked with just one type of dialect feature -- phonological variants that are intended to illustrate the typical accent of the South. The two primary markers are

deletion of post-vocalic [r]	--	father > fathaw
		artists > awtusts
		never > nevah
		your > yo'
		war > woe
		after > aftah
		perfectly > pofectly
		North > No'th
		Charlottesburg > Charlottesboag
		{Note that the first "r" remains.}
[ay] > [a:]	--	I > Ah
		my > mah
		like > lahke

It is interesting to note that no orthographic cluster reduction of the present progressive suffix occurs, which is commonly used to mark an informal or lower-class Southern accent.

Why does the daughter's speech contain four times the density of dialect markers than that of her father's speech? The Colonel is a businessman whose abilities in conducting his affairs have enabled him and motivated him to speak a more standard, less marked English. On the other hand, the daughter has fewer contacts outside her region; in addition, the Southern accent is considered charming among females.

Fulkerson and Beaton

Two characters who have major involvement with the publishing venture in New York are Fulkerson and Beaton. Fulkerson is a journalist from the West who becomes the business manager of the journal that hires Basil March as its editor. Beaton is an artist hired to do the artwork for the journal. Both characters have a low density of dialect markers in their speech. The following exchange between the men illustrates their speech (again with underlining indicating words that have been marked as dialectal):

> *Fulkerson*: "That's all right, ... Or if it isn't, we can make it. You and March will pull together first-rate. I don't care how much of the ideal you put into the thing; the more the better. I can look after the other end of the schooner myself."
> *Beaton*: "You don't understand me, ... I'm not trying to get a rise out of you. I'm in earnest. What you want is some man who can have patience with mediocrity putting on the style of genius, and with genius turning mediocrity on his hands. I haven't any luck with men; I don't get on with them; I'm not popular." (123)

Dialect markers can be identified in this passage in the form of lexical items, such as "pull together" and "get a rise." But no features are included here that mark either dialect as regional, ethnic, or nonstandard. In other passages, Fulkerson's speech does include a few such features, such as "ain't" and "baccy" (for *tobacco*). But these incidences are rare, and they are nonexistent in Beaton's language.

These characters are men of the humanities, men with whom Howells could relate personally. It is understandable that he would view their speech as being as close to standard as the speech of the Marches.

A Hazard of New Fortunes has more dialect marking in character dialogue than any other novel by Howells. The 1880's was his most productive decade in terms of writing critically acclaimed works. All the novels that are considered to be his best were written in this decade: *A Modern Instance* (1882), *The Rise of Silas Lapham* (1885), and *Indian Summer* (1886). And his final work from this decade -- *A Hazard of New Fortunes* -- is considered to be his crowning literary achievement, his most powerful and most socially minded novel. Not coincidentally, it is the novel in which he most effectively and most consistently uses literary dialect as a primary tool in establishing character. It is also the last of his fictional works to be hailed by critics.

"A Pair of Patient Lovers": Basil Tells the Story

Howells wrote two short stories in the mid-'90's that were narrated by Basil March. "A Circle in the Water" is a love story based on a father-daughter relationship. Unlike the works Howells had produced in the previous fifteen years, this tale has a syrupy ending.

"A Pair of Patient Lovers" is a love story that is structured within Howells's favorite setting for the Marches -- a trip. This time, they are off to retrace the leg of their wedding journey that took them into Canada. This story focuses on the relationship between Reverend Glendenning (an Episcopalian minister) and Miss Bentley, a young Bostonian. Their engagement is delayed and sabotaged by Miss Bentley's mother, an arrogant lady suffering from ill health. Miss Bentley is plagued by guilt that, by marrying Glendenning, she would be abandoning her mother. In the end, this tale also has a "live happily ever after" conclusion.

The language of the characters in this story is in marked contrast with the language of the people in *Hazard*. As the table presented earlier in this chapter shows, the dialect markers in the Marches' speech nearly disappear (.36%). That number pertains to both the dialogue and the narration of Basil. The dialogue of the other three characters in this story is equally free from dialect markers.

The stories written at this point in Howells's career may mark his first steps back into the realm of romanticism. They appear in the two to three years following the death of Howells's father in 1894. The lack of dialect may also be due to the types of characters in the story, characters Howells would either esteem (a minister) or see as speaking standard English (Bostonians).

Their Silver Wedding Journey: The Trek Back to Romanticism

Ten years after *Hazard*, the Marches make their final appearance in Howells's fiction in *Their Silver Wedding Journey*, once again off on a trip, this time to Europe. Their trip is a sabbatical for Basil from the rigors and stress of being an editor, which again mirrors real life for Howells. At age 62, Howells was beginning to feel like and see himself as an old man.

Howells had great difficulty in writing this novel. In a March 1898 letter to his sister, Aurelia, he wrote the following, which seems to imply a weariness with or a criticism of realism:

> I can't get the kind of grip I want on my story; everything is much more difficult than it used to be; but I keep trying. Sometimes I have to ask myself if my best days for writing are not past. I have written a great deal on the lines I attempted long ago; and I think the present novel will be the last I shall do on them. I am an elderly man, and I ought to deal more with things of spiritual significance. . . . Outer life no longer interests me as it once did, ... (*SL*, v. 4, 168)

These various aspects -- the Marches 25th wedding anniversary, weariness from a lifetime of stressful work, the end of the century, the deaths of his daughter and father, the invalidism of his wife, old age -- combined to revive Howells's more romantic perspective on life, and in this novel, the dialogue illustrates his steps towards a return (in some ways) to romantic literature. This novel -- though much longer than *Hazard* (which was itself a long novel) -- contains much less dialogue. It is a return to the style of *Their Wedding Journey*, more a novel of narrative impressions than Howells's novels of the previous two decades had been.

The speech of Basil and Isabel shows an inconsistency that is not found in previous works. In the first three works in which they appear, the style of their language changes from work to work, but within each work, their style is consistent. However, in this novel, the Marches waver between the very simple, realistic speech they used in *Hazard* to the more involved, romantic language they used when they first appeared in *Their Wedding Journey*. This curious combination of styles is illustrated in one short speech by Isabel. The underlined words and phrases illustrate the differing styles of language:

> I shouldn't feel so <u>shabby</u> if we *had* seen them. But to <u>hang round here</u> in this <u>plebeian abeyance</u>, and then to be defeated and defrauded at last! I wonder how long this sort of thing is going on? (334)

Basil also displays this curious mixture in a single sentence: "It's a <u>tough nut</u> for the <u>casuist</u> to <u>try his tooth on</u>" (400).

The words and phrases underlined (my underlining) illustrate the shifting of styles from casual and dialectic to more formal and even pompous. Such a combination of styles is certainly not uncommon in real speech, but it is not common in the previous speech of Basil and Isabel March. In earlier works, their speech was one way *or* the other; here it is one way *and then* the other.

As on their first wedding journey, the Marches meet and interact with a wide variety of characters with a variety of regional, ethnic, and professional backgrounds, and thus a variety of dialects. These are the primary characters the Marches encounter:

L. J. Burnamy -- a young journalist
Major Eltwin -- an elderly businessman from Ohio
General Triscoe -- a wealthy, discontented Civil War general and a very possessive father

Agatha Triscoe -- General Triscoe's daughter
Otterson -- a businessman from Iowa
Stoller -- a tyrannical tycoon from Chicago

All but two of these characters are given an unmarked dialect (with less than a 2% density of dialect features). The speech of the numerous Germans frequently encountered on the streets of Germany is depicted as standard English, similar to the German utterings of Landau in *Hazard*. The last two characters listed, Otterson and Stoller, are the primary dialect characters of this novel, and the density of markers in their speech is low compared to the dialect of characters in *Hazard*. The density of markers in Otterson's speech is 4.5%, and in Stoller's 5.5%. Such a low density would hardly even mark these characters as dialectal in *Hazard*, when compared to the densities of 28% for Lindau, 14% for Elizabeth Dryfoos, and 28% for Madison Woodburn. Yet with the majority of characters speaking a nearly unmarked dialect, Otterson and Stoller stand out as having a less-than-standard speech.

Why are these two characters given more dialect markers than the other characters in the novel? One reason might be that they are the two characters who come from west of Ohio -- Otterson from Iowa and Stoller from Illinois. In addition, Otterson is a rather unworldly, innocent, though cheerful, young man who is on his first trip abroad, while Stoller is the stereotypical ugly American businessman, a sour-natured tycoon who has achieved success by bullying people.

What do these five works in which the Marches appear illustrate about Howells's use of language with respect to his literary theories?

As was illustrated in previous chapters, Howells's commitment to realism developed gradually, growing out of a perspective that was initially more romantic. And as his realism became more deeply rooted in his writing, his concern with language became a more prominent characteristic of that realism. The works discussed here, with a focus on Howells's most recurring characters, illustrate Howells's growing use of realistic language as a tool for portraying the realism in his works, especially in developing his characters.

The final three decades of the 19th century were his most important literary years. During these years, he produced the literary and critical works that would permanently establish his place in American literature. It was during that time he became the "Dean" of this country's literary scene. And it was during that period that Basil and

Isabel March were his frequent literary companions. The Marches -- their experiences, their encounters, their acquaintances, and their language -- epitomize these same aspects of Howells's life and career.

As was stated earlier, the peak of Howells's literary achievements is *A Hazard of New Fortunes*. Many aspects -- plot, character, theme -- establish it as an important contribution to American literature. But the language of the novel, especially the dialect used to characterize the people, should give the novel a significant place in literary history in helping to establish the importance of literary dialect in establishing character, in giving the reader a sense of the people in the work.

Many critics hail *The Adventures of Huckleberry Finn* as the crowning achievement in the use of dialect in character development. But it should be noted that that same decade also gave the world *A Hazard of New Fortunes*, which is also a significant illustration of the effectiveness of using dialect features in developing and establishing character.

This analysis provides a telling illustration of Howells's interest in and reliance on language in developing his literary theories and sensibilities. The evolution of his use of literary dialect in his fiction written in the last three decades of the nineteenth century illustrates his reliance on linguistic devices in developing his brand of realistic fiction. Analysis of works from this period also gives interesting evidence of his linguistic attitudes by illustrating how and to whom he provided dialect in his works.

In the end, a study of Howells is incomplete without attention to his attitudes towards language. As the last few chapters have shown, his theory of fiction is intertwined with his theory of language. The two cannot be separated. And the single aspect studied here -- literary dialect -- provides solid evidence of the intertwining of these two aspects.

CHAPTER 6

Howells on Stage: Realism in Drama

I want you in acting to make note of any
little turns that will improve [the diction].
Howells to Lawrence Barrett, 1877

In addition to his enormous output of fiction and criticism, Howells also wrote thirty-six plays. His desire to write for the stage developed early in his life; he wrote his first play before he became a teenager. So it was natural for him to turn to drama once he had established himself in the literary circles of New England.

His career as a dramatist started in 1874 -- two years after the appearance of *Their Wedding Journey* -- with a fairly straightforward translation (not an adaptation) of *Sansone*, written by the Italian dramatist D'Aste. The poetic translation was hailed by critics, who praised the "literary finish" and the superiority of the diction of Howells's work. But Howells quickly began to argue against the use of such poetic diction in drama.

As he became more comfortable with the dramatic form, his approach to that genre mirrored his approach to fiction. As Walter J. Meserve, a drama historian, notes, "Howells's theory of drama was simply a logical extention [sic] of his theory of fiction with the added qualifications made necessary by the limitations of the drama" (*Outline*, 140-41). In other words, Howells's plays were, for the most part, filled with realistic detail, contemporary references and allusions, and characters based on his own friends and acquaintances. And he insisted that "[p]eople speak 'naturally' on the stage, even if that meant that the play would be full of colloquialisms, dialects, or vulgarities" (Richardson, 156). Meserve feels that "[o]ne of Howells's major strengths in the drama was his ability to depict brilliant conversation -- far more witty and clever than anything being written in American drama of this time" (*Outline*, 155). And Howells worked to make that conversation realistic, the "real" language of the "real" characters being depicted. As Gary Richardson notes,

> Just as the subjects of realistic plays were to be derived from "real life" and the representation was to be structured . . . by the rhythms derived from an "objectively" observed flow of the events themselves, so too the diction and dialogue of the characters must do nothing to destroy the illusion that the audience was hearing human beings in everyday life. (156)

Howells recognized this need and worked to eliminate what he felt were the romantic characteristics of the language on stage -- lyricism, rhetorical flourishes, asides, and soliloquies -- from the American drama during his career.

But as was the case in other areas of his work, Howells was self-contradictory. Meserve notes that Howells "occasionally slipped from his throne of realism and cavorted with the romantics" (*Outline*, 193). Howells wrote four poetic dramas: *Yorick's Love* (1878), *Priscilla* (1879), *A Sea Change or Love's Stowaway* (1884), and *The Mother and the Father* (1900). Ironically, Howells's greatest financial success on the stage was *Yorick's Love*, which violated almost every aesthetic principle he espoused for realistic drama.

Howells's dramatic works also mirror his fiction in one important structural way -- a married couple (the Robertses) that was patterned on him and his wife appear in one-third (twelve) of his plays, similar to the frequent appearances of the Marches, who were also patterned after him and his wife. The Robertses are accompanied by another married couple (the Campbells), who are based loosely on Mark Twain and his wife. These couples appear in the following plays (which some critics feel can be approached as a single twelve-act play):

The Sleeping Car (1882)
The Elevator (1884)
The Garrisons (1885)
The Mouse Trap (1886)

Five-O'clock Tea (1887)
A Likely Story (1888)
The Albany Depot (1889)
Evening Dress (1892)
A Letter of Introduction (1892)
The Unexpected Guests (1893)
A Masterpiece of Diplomacy (1894)
The Smoking Car (1898)

These plays are among Howells's best-known, and Meserve contends that a study of these twelve works provides the most elucidating analysis of Howells's total dramatic production.

The March-Roberts similarities are helpful in establishing a basis for a comparison between Howells's attitudes and practices in the different genres. In particular for this study, the two couples allow a comparison of the use of dialect within the dialogue of these couples, as well as in the dialogue of the characters with whom they interact.

In general, drama would seem to call for less literary dialect than fiction does, since dramatists can issue instructions for how a character should speak. And though, according to Meserve, the speeches in Howells's plays "were loaded with commonplace phrases and the overused expressions of average conversation" (*Outline*, 141), Howells presents very little dialect. Of the twelve plays listed above, five were selected for a close analysis of the dialogue -- the first and last plays and three in between, which were written at approximately equal intervals:

The Sleeping Car (1882)
The Mouse Trap (1886)
The Albany Depot (1889)
The Unexpected Guests (1893)
The Smoking Car (1898)

The findings can be generalized for all five. Very little dialect exists, and what dialect is presented has racial or ethnic roots.

The primary characters -- the Robertses and the Campbells -- consistently have a density of dialect markers under two percent (usually under one percent). In fact, Mr. Roberts (who is based on Howells himself) has no dialect markers in his speech. Their friends and relatives also have similar density percentages. In these five plays, only three characters could be labeled as dialect characters:

* The porter in *The Sleeping Car*:

This character is clearly an African-American, though no specific identification is given. But the markers in his speech indicate his race, at least according to the way Howells chose to represent certain features of the dialect. Nearly 20% of the words in this character's dialogue are marked with a dialect feature. Examples include the following:

-- *phonological features*:

[Δ] > [d]	"de ladies' trunks dere"
	"hang deir bonnets"
post-vocalic [r] deletion	"Yes, sah"
consonant cluster reduction	"gen'leman"
	"Jes' like"

-- grammatical errors:

nonstandard verb forms	"dey was boys and girls"
	"dat lady's took de hook"

-- lexical items: "routing" meaning "waking" or "rousting"

*Mrs. McIlheny, an Irish cook, and (3) her husband in *The Albany Depot*:

The McIlhenys are poor, working-class immigrants. The husband has much more dialogue than the wife, though both have a high density of dialect markers -- hers is 24%, while his is 32%. The vast majority of the features that appear in their dialogue are phonological, representing the accented English of an Irish dialect, similar to the written representation of the German-tinged English of Lindau in *A Hazard of New Fortunes*. In fact, the density of markers in Lindau's speech is remarkably similar to those of the McIlhenys -- 28%, which is just the average between the Irish couples' percentages. With Howells, this similarity is most likely no coincidence. He must have recognized how far a writer could go in representing nonstandard phonological features in dialogue without challenging the comprehension or the patience of his audience.

The dialect of the McIlhenys is primarily depicted through phonological features, as illustrated in the following passages. Again, the words that are marked with a dialect feature have been underlined.

> *McIlheny*: And are ye the mahn that's after takun' my wife for yer enke?
> *Mrs. Mc.*: And there's the other wan I saw jokun' wid 'um, and puttin' um up to it.
> *McIlheny*: That's what ye're after thinkun', Mary; but I haven't got annything to do with what ye're after thinkun'. All I wannt to know is what this mahn meant by preshumin' to speak to a lady he didn't know, and takun' her for a cuke.

Of all the dialogue and dialects analyzed for this study, the dialect markers in the speech of the McIlhenys is the most challenging to sort and to classify. Though the density is similar to that of Lindau, the number of different types of features is higher.

Despite the fact that the porter and the McIlheneys are secondary characters, their dialect illustrates the fact that Howells was willing and able to depict dialect in the speech of his stage characters when he felt the need or urge to do so. In these twelve plays, which are generally recognized as his best dramatic work, he apparently felt that need or urge rarely.

Howells adapted three of his novels for the stage: *A Foregone Conclusion, The Rise of Silas Lapham*, and *A Hazard of New Fortunes*. It is enlightening to examine the depiction of dialect in these adaptations to see how Howells's usage of literary dialect in drama compares with that in his fiction. Since this study has already examined the dialect in *Hazard*, this is the logical adaptation to analyze here.

This adaptation, which was completed ten years after the publication of the novel, was actually a collaboration between Howells (an aging author losing a grip on his motivation and desire to write) and Frank Drake, a young New York newspaperman. Drake actually approached Howells to request permission to write an adaptation of *The Rise of Silas Lapham*. Since Howells had already done that and had met with no success in selling it, he suggested to Drake that they work together to adapt *Hazard*. This duo had no more success getting their version of *Hazard* to the stage, and only parts of this work are extant. However, enough of the work is still available to illustrate the types of changes made to the language of the characters.

In general, few changes are made. The characters who have a low density of dialect markers in their speech in the novel still have a low density in the play. The characters who had high density in the novel have a high density in the play. In fact, Howells and Drake cut and pasted parts of the novel directly into the stage version. But some changes were made:

* In Lindau's German accent, "tventy" was changed to "twenty."
* In the novel, Lindau's pronunciation of *live* is written as "life." In the play, this word remains the same the first time it appears, but the second time Lindau says the word, it is written as "leefe".
* Lindau never utters a German word in the novel. In the play, he bids March farewell by saying "Auf Wiedersehen"; March even repeats the phrase.
* Instances of eye dialect disappear, which makes sense since eye dialect is a visual device for depicting dialect, making it useless in a stage play. In the novel, one of the Dryfoos girls says, "We staid three years." The play changes that to "stayed."
* In the speech of Elizabeth Dryfoos, the spelling of *ain't* is regularized. The novel presents it with an "h" at times; the play does not.

The other dialect character, Madison Woodburn, does not appear in the parts of the play that still exist.

These changes are comparatively minor compared to the types of changes that could have been made. Essentially, the literary dialect in this adaptation -- as well as the dialect in the series of twelve plays discussed earlier in this chapter -- shows little distinction between Howells's approach to dialogue in fiction and in drama. And while Meserve may claim that the speech in Howells's plays is "loaded with commonplace phrases and the overused expressions of average conversation" (*Outline*, 141), these "commonplace phrases" and "overused expressions" are still standard rather than dialectal usage.

In 1891, in *Criticism and Fiction*, Howells wrote that literature "which seeks only to entertain need not be held so strictly to the tenets of realistic fiction" (48-49). In the entire canon of Howells's works -- the fiction, the poetry, the criticism, and the dramas -- it could be argued that his one-act farces, such as the series of twelve discussed in this chapter, are his only works that set out to be nothing more than light entertainment, with no literary or social significance. Thus, he was willing to ease his commitment to realism for these plays. Yet, they are very realistic. And ironically, some of his works that set out to be much more than simply entertaining are those that end up violating his ideals of realism. That is yet another contradiction in Howells's career.

In the end, Howells deserves a better reputation as a dramatist than he now has. Gary Richardson notes that Howells's influence on contemporary dramatists and the audiences of the day cannot be overestimated. He offers this summation of Howells's plays: "[T]here are no 'great actions,' but the actions presented resonate with the lived experience of their readers and viewers. The plays are, in a word, real" (162).

CHAPTER 7

The Final Years: The Dean's Return to Romanticism

Certainly it is hard to please every man,
because of diversity and change of language.
William Caxton (in his preface to the *Aenid)*

After the turn of the century, Howells's life -- both personal and literary -- changed dramatically. Though, in the final decade of the 19th century, he had lost his daughter and his father, the first decade of the new century was to decimate his social world. In the span of nine years, he lost many of the people with whom he had the closest relationships: John Fiske in 1901, John Hay in 1905, Thomas Bailey Aldrich in 1907, Charles Eliot Norton and Edmund Clarence Stedman in 1908, Richard Watson Gilder and Edward Everett Hale in 1909. But the year following was even more tragic for Howells. In April 1910, he received word that his closest friend and literary comrade, Mark Twain, had died. Just two weeks later, his life's companion -- Elinor Mead Howells -- was dead.

This first decade of the new century was to be the worst of Howells's personal life, and it was to be his final decade as an influential force in American letters. Between 1901 and 1912, he received honorary doctorate degrees from Yale, Oxford, Columbia, and Princeton. And in 1904, he was selected as one of the first seven members -- and the first president -- of the American Academy of Arts and Letters. In 1911, a special Library Edition of his works was begun, with eleven volumes eventually being published.

But these honors were to constitute what could be called Howells's final hurrah as a living writer. In the last two decades of his life, his literary output slowed, though into his seventies, he still managed to produce over half a dozen book-length works, numerous articles and reviews, a new regular column, and several plays. However, the quality of that output, especially the fiction and the dramas, did not match the critical successes he had had during the 1880's and 1890's.

The late 1890's and the early years of the twentieth century saw the emergence of a new generation of writers who had been weaned on the realism of Howells but who were not content to accept what they perceived as a literary theory that was too genteel. Hamlin Garland, Stephen Crane, Theodore Dreiser, Jack London, and Frank Norris were coming onto the scene, and though Howells was a strong influence in the development of their literary attitudes, he also was the primary representative of a literary movement and ideology that seemed outdated and unsatisfactory for the new century. Not only was Howells the epitome of 19th-century realism, but in his final years, he also showed signs of returning to the romantic tendencies he had shown in his early career. Critical recognition of Howells's dual tendencies towards realism and romanticism at different points in his career appeared in several reviews and critical comments that appeared in the early part of this century. Among the numerous comments, these two tributes written upon the occasion of Howells's death illustrate that critical recognition:

> Though he scorned the "romance," and accepted the name of "realist," he never for a moment was merely the realist. (*Boston Evening Transcript*, 13)

> [Howells was] a victim of a Frankenstein Monster that he helped to call into existence -- caught between traditional romance and continental realism. (*New York Tribune*, 12)

As Chapter 5 illustrated in the study of Howells's use of dialect, he was straying away from hardcore realism towards the end of the 19th century. With the deaths of so many family members and close friends, growing older and lonelier with the passing years, Howells returned to the romanticism of his youth and early career. Such a psychological reaction to old age and loss of loved ones is certainly understandable. But in the context of the literary movement of the times, this return to romanticism is surprising.

With the growing proliferation of works that presented a more naturalistic version of realism, it would have been easy for Howells to adopt the pessimistic fatalism of naturalism. Perhaps the timing of naturalism's emergence affected this direction of Howells's final years. Would Howells have turned towards naturalism had it emerged, say, in 1917, following the death of Henry James, whom he considered his last good friend on the planet? But the early naturalistic works appeared well before Howells began to lose his loved ones. Though 1900 is commonly identified as the starting date of the period of naturalism, Garland's *Main-Travelled Roads* (1891) and *Jason Edwards* (1892) are considered by some to be the earliest works of Naturalism (Ahnebrink, 411). Crane's "Maggie: A Girl of the Streets" was published in 1893. Dreiser's *Sister Carrie* appeared in 1900, as did London's collection of stories, *The Son of the Wolf.*

As these early naturalistic works appeared, Howells was still a critical force, and he resisted the harsh, pessimistic realism of those writers. His dislike for naturalism was already entrenched before his own life took its turn towards a harsher reality.

The attitudes of these naturalists towards Howells were ones of both admiration and rejection. Garland considered Howells a friend and colleague. Crane saw him as a literary model and sponsor. Norris viewed Howells as the only substantive writer that this country had produced in the late 19th century. But just as Howells had rejected and fought against the romanticism in his early career -- despite his admiration of its leading writer, Nathaniel Hawthorne -- so these naturalists were rejecting and fighting against 19th century realism despite their admiration for its leading proponent. This rejection was epitomized by comments of Crane and Sinclair Lewis.

Despite their rejection of Howells, these men were his literary heirs, and they did not completely reject their inheritance. Their literary theories and their literary language were both affected by the fiction and criticism of Howells. In an 1891 piece in the *New York Tribune*, Crane wrote,

> No man stands for a more vital principle than does Mr. Howells. He stands for modern spirit, sympathy and truth. . . . He does not insist upon any special material, but only that the novelist be true to himself and to the things he sees. . . . He stands for all that is progressive and humanitarian in our fiction, and his following increases each day. (5)

In his short biography of Crane, Edwin Cady claimed that the young naturalist-to-be, like Howells, had “a tentative conversion” from “a neo-romanticism to Howells' realism" (98). The 1890's were not kind to Crane's impression of Howells. Despite the fact that Howells had helped Crane at a time when the young writer was ready to abandon his craft, Crane's opinion of Howells eventually became one of open professional dislike. In 1900, shortly before his death, Crane offered what proved to be his final assessment of Howells, in response to Howells's being nominated as the first member of the newly forming American Academy of Arts and Letters:

> The name of W. D. Howells occurs to somebody. But, no; he wears collars. It is known; it is common talk. He has never had his photograph taken while enwrapped in a carelessly negligent bath towel. In the name of God, let us have virility; let us look for the wild, free son of nature. ("Stephen Crane Says", 8)

In 1901, an essay by Frank Norris pondered the question of an American School of Fiction. Of all the writers he mentions in that essay, Howells alone survived the assessment:

> Mr. Howells alone is left, ... Of all producers of American fiction he has had the broadest vision, at once a New Englander and a New Yorker, an Easterner and -- in the Eastern sense -- a Westerner. But . . . Mr. Howells has had no successors. (196)

That final remark is a telling comment in that works by Norris's fellow naturalists Crane, London, and Dreiser had all found print by this time.

Norris also wrote "A Plea for Romantic Fiction," in which he asks, "Why should it be that so soon as the novelist addresses himself -- seriously -- to the consideration of contemporary life he must abandon Romance and take up that harsh, loveless, colourless, blunt tool called Realism?" (214). That query pointedly illustrates the naturalists' dissatisfaction with Howells's brand of Realism. Norris goes on to elaborate that point:

> Realism stultifies itself. It notes only the surface of things. For it, Beauty is not even skin deep, but only a geometrical plane, without dimensions and depth, a mere outside. Realism is very excellent so far as it goes, but it goes no further than the Realist himself can actually see, or actually hear. Realism is minute; it is the drama of a broken teacup, the tragedy of a walk down the block, the excitement of an afternoon call, the adventure of an invitation to dinner. It is the visit to

> my neighbour's house, a formal visit, from which I may draw no conclusions. I see my neighbor and his friends -- very, oh, such very probable people -- and that is all. Realism bows upon the doormat and goes away and says to me, as we link arms on the sidewalk: 'That is life.' And I say it is not. It is not, as you would very well see if you took Romance with you to call upon your neighbor. (215-216)

Those comments show Norris's straying away from Howellsian realism, but his comments on "Simplicity in Art" sound similar to those of Howells:

> The mistake that we little people are so prone to make is this: that the more intense the emotional quality of the scene described, the more "vivid," the more exalted, the more richly coloured we suppose should be the language.
>
> When the crisis of the tale is reached there is where we like the author to spread himself, to show the effectiveness of his treatment. But if we would only pause to take a moment's thought we must surely see that the simplest, even the barest statement of fact is only not all-sufficient but all-appropriate. (243)

These comments remind us of Howells's comments regarding the distinction between the language of romanticism and the language of realism. He wanted literary language to be real, simple, natural; the language of romanticism was anything but that.

Sinclair Lewis's sarcastic comments in his Nobel Prize acceptance speech represent one of the most well known literary attacks on Howells:

> It was with the emergence of William Dean Howells that we first began to have something like a standard, and a very bad standard it was. Mr. Howells was one of the gentlest, sweetest and most honest of men and had the code of a pious old maid whose greatest delight is to have tea at the vicarage. He abhorred not only profanity and obscenity, but all of what Wells called the jolly coarseness of life. In his fantastic vision of life farmers, seamen and factory hands may exist, but the farmer must never be covered with muck, the seaman must never roll out bawdy chanteys, and all of them must long for an opportunity to visit Florence and smile quaintly at the quaintness of the beggars.
>
> [Howells] actually was able to take Mark Twain . . . and put that fiery old savage into an intellectual frock coat and top hat. . . . He is still worshiped by Hamlin Garland, an author who should have been in every way greater than Howells, but who, under Howells's influence, changed from a harsh and magnificent realist into a genial, insignificant lecturer . . . .

> . . . Dreiser more than any other man, marching alone, usually unappreciated, often hated, has cleared the trail from Victorian and Howellsian timidity and gentility in American fiction to honesty and boldness and passion of life. Without his pioneering, I doubt if any of us could, unless we liked to be sent to jail, seek to express life and beauty and terror. (quoted in Cady & Frazier, 153)

Lewis's attitude towards Howells was based on certain misconceptions common at the time, but as Lewis's biographer, Mark Schorer, points out, there were deep-seated similarities between these two seemingly dissimilar writers:

> . . . Howells's middle-class liberal optimism was so much like Lewis's own, his social criticism, again like Lewis's, deeply tempered by it. Both, steering a clear line between a surly proletariat and a stuffed plutocracy, wished to assure the middle class that the promise of American life lay in its best values. Savage and boisterous as Lewis's writing was sometimes to be, his reticences about sex and the turmoil of the subjective life were Howells's too. (231)

Schorer recognized the fact that, though Lewis rebelled against Howellsian realism, he was at the same time a product of it in many ways. Schorer saw Lewis's emergence on the literary scene significant in its timing:

> [Lewis] became through this single book the spokesman for a literary generation, and the year 1920 is in this sense historic. American culture seems always to have had a literary spokesman, a single writer who presented American culture and American attitudes towards its culture, to the world. The last of these had been William Dean Howells, who died in the spring of 1920, ancient and honored. The summer gaped; autumn brought *Main Street*. And no writer since Howells has more nearly approximated his position than Lewis, ... (270)

In his relation to Howells, Lewis was a literary representative for his generation of writers. Dreiser, London, Norris, Crane, Fitzgerald, Faulkner, Hemingway, Steinbeck -- all were like Lewis in their rejection of the "gentle and quiet realism" of Howells, yet all display in their works a realistic approach to subject matter and a plainness of speech that were undoubtedly affected by Howells. Few of them ever recognized or admitted it. In fact, in the biographies and collections of letters of all but Norris and Crane, Howells is never even mentioned. Once he was no longer living (and to some people years before his death), he was seen as inconsequential, his lasting effects as negligible. But in truth, he was anything but inconsequential.

The one writer of the 20th century who was more than willing to sing the praises of Howells was Robert Frost. In 1921, Frost wrote to Garland, acknowledging his debt to Howells:

> My obligation to him . . . is not for the particular things he did in verse form, but for the perennial poetry of all his writings in all forms. I learned from him a long time ago that the loveliest theme of poetry was the voices of people. No one ever had a more observing ear or clearer imagination for the tones of those voices. No one ever brought them more freshly to book. He recorded them equally with actions, indeed as if they were actions (and I think they are). (quoted in Thompson, 265)

This comment was not merely a momentary tribute paid to Howells shortly after his death. Frost was deeply indebted to Howells for helping the poet shape his attitudes towards poetic language. Frost saw the need for poetry to rely more on the usage of the vernacular and less on unnatural formal English. In the decade before Howells's death, Frost's frequent comments on the language of poetry sounded a lot like Howells's decades earlier:

> *Letter to Sidney Cox, 1914* :
>
> . . . you cant [sic] read a single good sentence with the salt in it unless you have previously heard it spoken. Neither can you with the help of all the characters and diacritical marks pronounce a single word unless you have previously heard it actually pronounced. (quoted in Barry, 62)
>
> *Letter to John Bartlett, 1914* :
>
> The most original writer only catches [sounds] fresh from talk, where they grow spontaneously. (quoted in Barry, 64)
>
> *Letter to E. A. Robinson, 1915* :
>
> It is good writing, or better than that, good speaking caught alive -- every sentence of it. The speaking tones are all there on the printed page, ... And the action is in the speech where it should be . . . . (quoted in Barry, 94)

Lecture to the Browne and Nichols School, 1915:

> . . . the Sounds in the mouths of men I found to be the basis of all effective expression. (quoted in Barry, 143)

Letter to Lewis N. Chase, 1917 :

> Someone had complained that a little thing of mine was "too near the level of talk." I didn't see why it shouldn't be. . . . I can't keep up any interest in sentences that don't SHAPE *on some speaking tone* of voice. (quoted in Barry, 70)

Letter to Regis Michaud, 1918:

> All writing, I don't care how exalted, how lyrical, or how seemingly far removed from the dramatic, must be . . . colloquial. . . .(quoted in Barry, 97)

Lecture to the Browne and Nichols School, 1918:

> There are two kinds of language: the spoken language and the written language -- our everyday speech which we call the vernacular; and a more literary, sophisticated, artificial, elegant language that belongs to books. We often hear it said that a man talks like a book in this second way. We object to anybody's talking in this literary, artificial English; we don't object to anybody's writing in it; we rather expect people to write in a literary, somewhat artificial style. I, myself, could get along very well without this bookish language altogether. I agree with the poet who visited this country not long ago when he said that all our literature has got to come down, sooner or later, to the talk of everyday life. William Butler Yeats says that all our words, phrases, and idioms to be effective must be in the manner of everyday speech.
>
> We've got to come down to this speech of everyday, to begin with -- the hard everyday word of the street, business, trades, work in summer . . . . (quoted in Barry, 145)

These comments are so similar to Howells's that they could be mistaken for Howells's own commentary, especially the comment about the "Sounds in the mouths of men," which is exactly where Howells urged writers of the 1880's to seek the most appropriate language for literature. Frost was certainly in the minority of Howells's successors in proudly proclaiming his debt to the aging realist. More of them were like Lewis, claiming to reject the man who actually helped shape their fiction in more ways than they cared to admit.

In 1891, Howells may have forecast the ultimate fate of his brand of realism. In *Criticism and Fiction*, he made an interesting connection between romanticism and realism:

> The romance of that day and the realism of this are in a certain degree the same. Romance then sought, as realism seeks now, to widen the bounds of sympathy, to level every barrier against aesthetic freedom, to escape from the paralysis of tradition. It exhausted itself in this impulse; and it remained for realism to assert that fidelity to experience and probability of motive are essential conditions of a great imaginative literature. It is not a new theory, but it has never before universally characterized literary endeavor. When realism becomes false to itself, when it heaps up facts merely, and maps life instead of picturing it, realism will perish too. (15)

The new generation of writers saw realism -- at least Howells's brand of it -- as "heaping up facts merely." They saw little realism beyond that, and thus no real relevance to the world.

Howells also provided what time has proved to be an accurate critical assessment of his literary tendencies, though he was writing of Emile Zola at the time:

> Zola embodied his ideal inadequately, as every man who embodies an ideal must. His realism was his creed, which he tried to make his deed; but, before his fight was ended, and almost before he began to forebode it a losing fight, he began to feel and to say . . . that he was too much a romanticist by birth and tradition, to exemplify realism in his work. He could not be all to the cause he honored . . . because his intellectual youth had been nurtured on the milk of romanticism at the breast of his mother-time. He grew up in the day when the great novelists and poets were romanticists, and what he came to abhor he had first adored. He was that pathetic paradox, a prophet who cannot practise [sic] what he preaches, who cannot build his doctrine into the edifice of a living faith. (*Prefaces*, 90)
>
> ********
>
> . . . He was bred if not born in the worship of the romantic, but his native faith was not proof against his reason, as again his reason was not proof against his native faith. He preached a crusade against romanticism, and fought a long fight with it, only to realize at last that

> he was himself too romanticistic to succeed against it, and heroically to own his defeat. (*Prefaces*, 100)

Those comments effectively summarize many of the inconsistencies and seeming contradictions in Howells's career. A man born into the romantic period grew to accept realism as the preferred method of literature, only to have to battle against his initial "in-bred" preferences -- Howells, the one figure who is regarded as the primary proponent and most steadfast defender of realism, the man who has been attacked as having been little more than a literary reporter stating the "facts and nothing but the facts," the man who has been accused of being a prudish censor of his fellow writers. In actuality, he was all of that and none of that. His career, like his character, was far too complex and far-reaching to analyze easily and describe quickly with sweeping generalizations.

The most accurate and fair statement that can be made of Howells is one that could be applied to any person who has stood at the forefront of a new theoretical movement -- the theory is easier to put into words than into practice. In other words, "easier said than done!"

More contemporary viewpoints of Howells and his career are beginning to approach him with more of a willingness to evaluate the man's work for what it accomplished, not for how closely it adhered to his own critical pronouncements of literary method. In the end, that approach will yield a more positive and meaningful estimation of Howells as a novelist and dramatist. Perhaps his reputation as a writer may one day equal his career as a critic. In many ways, they were separate careers involving separate men.

In his comments about Zola, Howells wrote, "To me his literary history is very pathetic" (*Prefaces*, 100). Certainly writers and critics who succeeded Howells felt the same about him. But neither man had a career or "literary history" that should be labeled pathetic. They may each have strayed from the path they set for themselves. But what resulted from that straying has been as important and meaningful for the literary histories of each man's country as their writings that did not stray.

Howells was a realist whose career ebbed and flowed in its realism. That is neither condemnable nor undesirable. It is real.

APPENDIX

Analyzing Howells's Literary Dialect

> The writer of a literary dialect is not concerned with giving an exact picture of the folklore of speech. As an artist, he must always keep his eye on the effect . . . .
>
> *George Phillip Krapp*

Chapter 5 presents the results of an analysis of the speech of the characters from selected works by Howells. This appendix presents illustrative examples of how that analysis was conducted.

Based generally on the methods of Alvin Gregg in his studies of William Faulkner's literary dialect, this analysis centered on the identification of dialect markers. For the purposes of this study, the term *dialect* is used to refer to any feature of a character's speech that Howells would have considered as marked or non-standard based on his own personal perceptions of standard English. (This notion is based on Sumner Ives's theory of literary dialect, which was summarized in Chapter 5.)

Specifically, this analysis was conducted as follows. First, representative passages of dialogue for each of the characters studied were selected. The total number of words in each passage were counted, and then also counted were those words and phrases marked with some type of dialect feature based on grammatical, phonological, lexical, or orthographical variations from the norm -- Howells's norm. Those variations were not categorized in detail. For example, social dialect features (such as the use of double negatives) were not distinguished from regional ones (such as the use of *y'all*) and stylistic ones (such as the contrast between formal and informal registers).

What follows are samples of these analyses for this study. The passages are excerpts from the dialogue of Basil March, whose speech is relatively free of dialect markers, as well as from the dialogue of two dialect characters from *A Hazard of New Fortunes*. In each passage, the underlined words or phrases are those that I were identified as being marked with a dialect feature.

Basil March, *Their Wedding Journey*

> Yes, I can't account for him except as the ghost of Southern travel, and I can't help feeling a little sorry for him. I suppose that almost any evil commends itself by its ruin; the wrecks of slavery are fast growing a fungus crop of sentiment, and they may yet outflourish the remains of the feudal system in the kind of poetry they produce. The impoverished slaveholder is a pathetic figure, in spite of all justice and reason; the beaten rebel does move us to compassion, and it is of no use to think of Andersonville in his presence. This gentleman, and others like him, used to be the lords of our summer resorts. They spent the money they did not earn like princes; they held their heads high; they trampled upon the Abolitionist in his lair; they received the homage of the doughface in his home. They came up here from their rice-swamps and cotton-fields, and bullied the whole busy civilization of the North. Everybody who had merchandise or principles to sell truckled to them, and travel amongst us was a triumphal progress. Now they're moneyless and subjugated (as they call it), there's none so poor to do them reverence, and it's left for me, an Abolitionist from the cradle, to sigh over their fate. After all, they had noble traits, and it was no great wonder they got to despise us, seeing what most of us were. It seems to me I should like to know our friend. I can't help feeling towards him as towards a fallen prince, heaven help my craven spirit! I wonder how our colored waiter feels towards him. I dare say he admires him immensely.

No words were marked as having a dialect feature. Thus, the dialect density of this passage is 0%. Certain words could be seen as illustrating a very formal (perhaps overly formal), standard dialect, such as *doughface*, *truckled*, and *amongst*. However, though these words are not in common usage now, they were more common examples of standard English in Howells's day.

Basil March, "Niagra Revisited"

> They are safe; they have no money. They are frugally confining themselves to the admiration of the Japanese bows and arrows yonder. Why have our Indians taken to making Japanese bows and arrows?

One lexical item out of thirty-three words gives this passage a density of 3%. The dialect feature here, as in the following passage, is lexical. On the rare occasions that Howells inserts a dialect feature in March's speech, it is a lexical variant. The more marked features -- the phonological variants -- he reserves for his dialect characters. In his mind, since he modeled March after himself, he naturally considered March's pronunciation as standard, based on his personal pronunciation.

Basil March, *A Hazard of New Fortunes*

> Well, of course there were mitigating circumstances. I could see that Fulkerson meant to keep the whip-hand himself, and that was reassuring. And besides, if the Reciprocity Life should happen not to want my services any longer, it wouldn't be quite like giving up a certainty; though, as a matter of business, I let Fulkerson get that impression; I felt rather sneaking to do it. But, if the worst comes to worst, I can look about for something to do in Boston; and, anyhow, people don't starve on two thousand a year, though it's convenient to have five. The fact is, I'm too old to change so radically. If you don't like my saying that, then you are, Isabel, and so are the children. I've no right to take them from the home we've made, and to change the whole course of their lives, unless I can assure them of something, and I can't assure them of anything. Boston is big enough for us, and it's certainly prettier than New York. I always feel a little proud of hailing from Boston; my pleasure in the place mounts the farther I get away from it. But I do appreciate it, my dear. I've no more desire to leave it than you have. You may be sure that if you don't want to take the children out of the Friday afternoon class, I don't want to leave my library here, and all the ways I've got set in. We'll keep on. Very likely the company won't supplant me; and if it does, and Watkins gets the place, he'll give me a subordinate position of some sort. Cheer up, Isabel! I have put Satan and his angel, Fulkerson, behind me, and it's all right. Let's go in to the children.

This passage contains 299 words. Thirteen words are identifed as being marked with a dialect feature; all are lexical items. That results in a 4% density, little change from this character's earlier dialogue.

Berthold Lindau, *A Hazard of New Fortunes*

> Ah, my tear yo'ng friendt! Passil! Marge! Iss it you? . . .
> No; I'm all righdt. Only a lidtle lazy, and a lidtle eggonomigal. Idt's jeaper to stay in pedt sometimes as to geep a fire a-goin' all the time. Don't wandt to gome too hardt on the brafer Mann, you know: . . . . You remember? Heine? You readt Heine still? Who is your favorite boet now, Passil? You write some boetry yourself yet? No? Well, I am gladt to zee you. Brush those baperss off of that jair. Well, idt is goodt for zore eyess. How didt you findt where I life?

Lindau's speech has a much denser representation of dialect. With thirty-five of ninety-nine words marked with a dialect feature, this passage has a density of 35%. This character and the next one are Howells's two primary dialect characters. Notice that the features in their speech are all phonological variants, as opposed to the lexical variants used in March's speech. A character speaking English with a German accent and one speaking with a Southern accent would naturally have speech that noticeably contrasts with Howells's own pronunciation.

Miss Woodburn, *A Hazard of New Fortunes*

> Ah don't know what yo' mothah means by yo' ho'se not being in oddah. Ah'm a great ho'se-keepah mahself, and Ah mean what Ah say.
> Ah suppose you awe going to be a great awtust? Ah've a great notion to take a few lessons mahself. Who's yo' teachah? Well, it's just beautiful, Miss Leighton; it's grand. Ah suppose it's raght expensive, now? Mah goodness! we have to cyoant the coast so much nowadays it seems to me we do nothing but cyoant it. Ah'd like to bah something once without askin' the price.

This representation of Southern dialect has a density of 29%. Of ninety-three words, twenty-seven are marked with a dialect feature.

BIBLIOGRAPHY

Works Cited:

Adams, Charles Francis, ed. *The Works of John Adams, Second President of the United States . . . by His Grandson Charles Francis Adams*. Boston, 1852.

Ahnebrink, Lars. *The Beginnings of Naturalism in American Fiction, 1891-1903*. New York: Russell & Russell, Inc., 1961.

Barry, Elaine. *Robert Frost on Writing*. New Brunswick: Rutgers University Press, 1973.

Brooks, Van Wyck. *America's Coming of Age*. New York: Doubleday, 1958.

Bruce, William Cable, ed. *Benjamin Franklin, Self-Revealed*. Volume 2. New York: Putnam's Sons, 1923.

Cady, Edwin H. *Stephen Crane*. New York: Twayne Publishers, Inc., 1962.

Cady, Edwin H. and David L. Frazier, eds. *The War of the Critics over William Dean Howells*. New York: Row, Peterson and Company, 1962.

Cooper, James Fenimore. *The Prairie: A Tale*. New York: Hurd and Houghton, 1870.

Crane, Stephen. "Howells Discussed at Avon-By-The-Sea." *New York Tribune*, August 18, 1891: 5.

Emerson, Ralph Waldo. "Nature: Addresses and Lectures." in *The Complete Works of Ralph Waldo Emerson*. Volume 1. Boston: Houghton, Mifflin, and Company, 1903.

Firkins, Oscar W. *William Dean Howells: A Study*. Cambridge: Harvard University Press, 1924.

Fryckstedt, Olov W. *In Quest of America: A Study of Howells's Early Development as a Novelist*. New York: Russell and Russell, 1958.

Gibson, William M. *William Dean Howells*. Minneapolis: University of Minnesota Press, 1967.

Halfmann, Ulrich, ed. "Interviews with William Dean Howells." *American Literary Realism* 6 (1973).

Harder, Jayne Crane. "James Russell Lowell: Linguistic Patriot." *American Speech* 29: 180-86.

Howells, William Dean. *Criticism and Fiction*. New York: New York University Press, 1959.

--------------------. *Editor's Study*. Edited by James Simpson. Troy, NY: Whitston Publishing Company, 1983.

--------------------. *A Hazard of New Fortunes*. Bloomington: Indiana University Press, 1976.

--------------------. *Italian Journeys*. Boston: Houghton, Mifflin and Company, 1867.

--------------------. "My Favorite Novelist and His Best Book." *Munsey's Magazine* 17 (April 1897): 18-25.

--------------------. *My Literary Passions*. New York: Greenwood Press, 1895.

--------------------. *A Pair of Patient Lovers*. Freeport, NY: Books for Libraries Press, 1901.

--------------------. *Prefaces to Contemporaries, 1882-1920*. Gainesville: Scholars' Facsimilies and Reprints, 1957.

--------------------. *Selected Letters, Volume I: 1852-1872*. Bloomington: Indiana University Press, 1979.

--------------------. *Selected Letters, Volume II: 1873-1881*. Bloomington: Indiana University Press, 1979.

--------------------. *Selected Letters, Volume III: 1882-1891*. Bloomington: Indiana University Press, 1980.

--------------------. *Selected Letters, Volume IV: 1892-1901*. Bloomington: Indiana University Press, 1981.

--------------------. *Selected Letters, Volume V: 1902-1911*. Bloomington: Indiana University Press, 1983.

--------------------. *Selected Letters, Volume VI: 1912-1920*. Bloomington: Indiana University Press, 1983.

--------------------. *Suburban Sketches*. Freeport, NY: Books for Libraries Press, 1898.

--------------------. *Their Wedding Journey*. Greenwich, CT: Fawcett Publications, Inc., 1960

--------------------. *Venetian Life*. New York: AMS Press, 1971.

Ives, Sumner. "A Theory of Literary Dialect" in *A Various Language: Perspectives on American Dialect.* Edited by Juanita V. Williamson and Virginia M. Burke. New York: Holt, Rinehart and Winston, Inc.,1971. Pp. 145-77.

Johnson, Clifton. "The Writer and the Rest of the World." *Outlook* 49 (March 31, 1894): 580-82. [Reprinted in Halfmann.]

Lowell, James Russell. *The Complete Writings of James Russell Lowell.* Volume 3. Boston: Houghton, Mifflin and Company, 1904.

Magill, Frank N., ed. *Magill Surveys: American Novel, Brown to James.* Pasedena: Salem Press, Inc., 1980

Mathews, M. M. *The Beginnings of American English: Essays and Comments.* Chicago: University of Chicago Press, 1931.

Mencken, H. L. *The American Language: An Inquiry into the Development of English in the United States.* 4th ed. New York: A. Knopf, 1977.

-----------. *The American Language: Supplement I.* New York: A. Knopf, 1945.

Meserve, Walter J. *An Outline History of American Drama.* Totowa, NJ: Littlefield, Adams & Company, 1970.

Moss, Richard J. *Noah Webster.* Boston: Twayne Publishers, Inc., 1984.

Neal, John. *American Writers: A Series of Papers Contributed to Blackwood Magazine (1824-1825).* Ed. by Fred L. Pattee. Durham, NC: Duke University Press, 1937.

------------. *Rachel Dyer.* Gainesville: Scholars' Facsimiles & Reprints, 1964.

Nettels, Elsa. *Language, Race, and Social Class in Howells's America.* Lexington: University of Kentucky Press, 1988.

-----------. Personal correspondence. June 16, 1988.

Norris, Frank. *The Responsibilities of the Novelist and Other Literary Essays.* New York: Greenwood Press, 1902.

Ogilvie, John. *The Imperial Dictionary.* London: Blackie and Son, 1856.

Peck, Harry Thurston. "Living Critics: XII -- William Dean Howells." *The Bookman* 4 (February 1897): 529-547.

Piatt, James J. and William Dean Howells. *Poems of Two Friends.* Columbus: Follett, Foster & Company, 1860.

Reeve, Clara. *The Progress of Romance and the History of Charoba, Queen of Aegypt.* E. M. Magill, ed. New York: The Facsimile Text Society, 1930.

Reeves, John K. "Introduction" to *Their Wedding Journey*. Bloomington: Indiana University Press, 1968.

Richardson, Gary A. *American Drama From the Colonial Period Through World War I: A Critical History*. New York: Twayne Publishers Inc., 1993.

Schorer, Mark. *Sinclair Lewis: An American Life*. New York: McGraw-Hill, 1961.

Smith, Henry Nash and William M. Gibson, eds. *Mark Twain-Howells Letters:The Correspondence of Samuel L. Clemens and William D. Howells*. 2 vols. Cambridge: The Belknap Press of Harvard University Press, 1960.

Spencer, Benjamin T. *The Quest for Nationality: An American Literary Campaign*. Syracuse: Syracuse University Press, 1957.

Stallman, R. W. and Lillian Gilkes, eds. *Stephen Crane: Letters*. New York: New York University Press, 1960.

Thompson, Lawrence, ed. *Selected Letters of Robert Frost*. New York: Holt, Rinehart, Winston, 1964.

van Westrum, A. Schade. "Mr. Howells on Love and Literature." *Lamp* 28 (February 1904): 27-31. [Reprinted in Halfmann.]

Warfel, Harry R. *Noah Webster, Schoolmaster to America*. New York: Macmillan Co., 1936

Webster, Noah. *A Compendious Dictionary of the English Language*. (A facsimile of the 1806 edition). New York: Bounty Books, 1970.

------------. *An American Dictionary of the English Language*. Editions cited: 1828, 1856.

------------. *Dissertations on the English Language*. (A facsimile of the 1789 edition.) Gainsville: Scholars' Facsimiles and Reprints, 1951.

------------. *On Being American: Selected Writings, 1783-1828*. Ed. by Homer D. Babbidge, Jr. New York: Praeger Publishers, 1967.

White, Richard Grant. *Words and their Uses, Past and Present: A Study of the English Language*, 20th edition. Boston: Houghton Mifflin, 1892.

Whitman, Walt. *An American Primer*. Ed. by Horace Traubel Boston: Small, Maynard, 1904. P. 6

"William Dean Howells." *New York Tribune* (May 12, 1920): 12.

"William Dean Howells." *Boston Evening Transcript* (May 11, 1920): 13.

Wolfram, Walt. *Dialects and American English.* Englewood Cliffs: Prentice Hall, 1991.

Wortham, Thomas, ed. *The Early Prose Writings of William Dean Howells,1853-1861.* Athens: Ohio University Press, 1990.

Youmans, Gilbert, and Greg Stratman. "American English: The Transition from Colonialism to Independence." *The End of Anglo-America: Historical Essays in the Study of Cultural Divergence.* Edited by R. A. Burchell. Manchester: Manchester University Press, 1991.

Works Consulted:

Aaron, Daniel. "Howells 'Maggie'." *New England Quarterly* 38: 85-90.

Arms, George, Mary Bess Whidden and Gary Scharnhorst, eds. *Staging Howells: Plays and Correspondence with Lawrence Barrett.* Albuquerque: University of New Mexico Press, 1994.

Babcock, C. Merton, ed. *The Ordeal of American English.* Boston: Houghton Mifflin Co., 1961.

Bennett, George N. *William Dean Howells: The Development of a Novelist.* Norman: University of Oklahoma Press, 1959.

Bennett, Jacob. "George Savary Wasson's Approach to Dialect Writing." *American Speech* 54: 90-101.

Berryman, John. *Stephen Crane: A Critical Biography.* Rev. ed. New York: Farrar, Straus, Giroux, 1977.

Borus, Daniel H. *Writing Realism: Howells, James and Norris in the Mass Market.* Chapel Hill: University of North Carolina Press, 1989.

Bowdre, Paul H., Jr. "Eye Dialect as a Problem in Graphics." *Visible Language* 16: 177-83.

Bridgman, Richard. *The Colloquial Style in America.* New York: Oxford University Press, 1966.

Brooks, Van Wyck. *Howells: His Life and World.* New York: E. P. Dutton & Company, Inc., 1959.

Cady, Edwin H. *The Realist at War: The Mature Years, 1885-1920, of William Dean Howells.* Syracuse: Syracuse University Press, 1958.

------------. *The Road to Realism: The Early Years, 1837-1885, of William Dean Howells.* Syracuse: Syracuse University Press, 1956.

Carrington, George and Ildiko' de Papp Carrington. *Plots and Characters in the Fiction of William Dean Howells.* Hamden, CT: Archon Books, 1976.

Carter, Everett. *Howells and the Age of Realism.* Hamden, CT: Archon Books, 1966.

Cole, Roger W. "Literary Representation of Dialect: A Theoretical Approach to the Artistic Problem." *The USF Language Quarterly* 24 (1986): 3-8.

Crowley, John W. *The Black Heart's Truth: The Early Career of W. D. Howells.* Chapel Hill: University of North Carolina Press, 1985.

--------------. *The Mask of Fiction: Essays on W. D. Howells.* Amherst: University of Massachusetts Press, 1989.

"Current Fiction." *Nation* 84, May 9, 1907: 434-35.

DeMille, G. E. "The Infallible Dean." *The Sewanee Review* 36, (April 1928): 148-56.

Eble, Kenneth E., ed. *Howells: A Century of Criticism.* Dallas: Southern Methodist University Press, 1962.

-----------------. *William Dean Howells*, 2nd edition. Boston: Twayne Publishers, 1982.

Eichelberger, Clayton L. *Published Comment on William Dean Howells Through 1920: A Research Bibliography.* Boston: G. K. Hall and Co., 1976.

Elliott, Fanny Mae and Lucy Clark, comps. *The Barrett Library, W. D. Howells: A Checklist of Printed and Manuscript Works of William Dean Howells in the Library of the University of Virginia.* Charlottesville: University of Virginia Press, 1959.

Ellison, Julie. *Emerson's Romantic Style.* Princeton: Princeton University Press, 1984.

Eschholz, Paul A., ed. *Critics on William Dean Howells.* Coral Gables: University of Miami Press, 1975.

Fine, Elizabeth. "In Defense of Literary Dialect: A Response to Dennis R. Preston." *Journal of American Folklore* 96: 323-30.

Grattan, C. Hartley. "Howells: Ten Years After." *American Mercury* 20, May 1930: 42-50.

Grebstein, Sheldon Norman. *Sinclair Lewis.* New York: Twayne Publishers, Inc., 1962.

Gregg, Alvin L. "Faulkner's Black Dialect and Literary Interpretation." Paper delivered at the Mid-America Linguistics Conference, 1983.

------------. "Faulkner's Changing Dialect Styles." Paper delivered at the Midwest American Dialect Society Session, MMLA Conference, 1983.

Gullason, Thomas Arthur. "New Light on the Crane-Howells Relationship." *New England Quarterly* 30: 389-92.

Howells, Mildred, ed. *Life in Letters of William Dean Howells*. 2 vols. New York: Russell and Russell, 1968.

Howells, William Dean. *A Chance Acquaintance*. Bloomington: Indiana University Press, 1971.

--------------------. *A Foregone Conclusion*. Boston: Houghton Mifflin Company, 1874.

--------------------. *Indian Summer*. Bloomington: Indiana University Press, 1971.

--------------------. *Literary Friends and Acquaintance: A Personal Retrospect of American Authorship*. Bloomington: Indiana University Press, 1968.

--------------------. *The Rise of Silas Lapham*. Bloomington: Indiana University Press, 1971.

--------------------. *Selected Literary Criticism, Volume I: 1859-1885.* Bloomington: Indiana University Press, 1993.

--------------------. *Selected Literary Criticism, Volume II: 1886-1897.* Bloomington: Indiana University Press, 1993.

--------------------. *Selected Literary Criticism, Volume III: 1898-1920.* Bloomington: Indiana University Press, 1993.

--------------------. *Their Silver Wedding Journey.* New York: Harper & Brothers, 1899.

--------------------. *Years of My Youth and Three Essays*. Bloomington: Indiana University Press, 1975.

Howells, William Dean, Henry James, et. al. *The Whole Family*. New York: Ungar Publishing Press, 1986.

James, Henry. *The Question of Our Speech*. Boston: Houghton Mifflin and Company, 1905

Kirk, Clara Marburg. *W. D. Howells and Art in His Time*. New Brunswick, NJ: Rutgers University Press, 1965.

Kirk, Clara Marburg and Rudolf Kirk. *William Dean Howells*. New Haven: College and University Press, 1962.

------------. *William Dean Howells: Representative Selections, with Introductions, Bibliography, and Notes*. New York: American Book Company, 1950.

Krapp, George Philip. *The English Language in America*. Volumes 1 and 2. New York: Ungar Publishing, 1925.

Lang, Andrew. "The New Fiction." *The Illustrated London News* 57 (August 3,1895): 141.

Lowell, James Russell. *The Biglow Papers*. Ed. by Thomas Wortham. DeKalb: Northern Illinois Press, 1977.

Lynn, Kenneth S. *William Dean Howells: An American Life*. New York: Harcourt Brace Jovanovich, Inc., 1970.

Macoun, Minnie. *Character and Comment Selected from the Novels of W. D. Howells*. Boston: Houghton, Mifflin and Company, 1889.

Marshall, Edward. "A Great American Writer." Philadelphia Press April 15, 1894: 27. [Reprinted in Halfmann.]

---------------. "The Greatest Living American Writer." *New York Press*. April 15, 1894.

Mathews, M. M. "American Character in American Fiction." *Munsey's Magazine* 44, August 1913: 794-98.

Mencken, H. L. "The Dean." *Prejudices: First Series*. New York: Alfred A. Knopf, 1919.

Meserve, Walter J. *The Complete Plays of William Dean Howells*. NewYork: New York University Press, 1960.

Miller, James E., Jr. *Walt Whitman*. Boston: Twayne Publishers, 1990.

Nettels, Elsa. *Language and Gender in American Fiction: Howells, James, Wharton, and Cather*. Charlottesville: University Press of Virginia, 1997.

-----------. "William Dean Howells and the American Language." *New England Quarterly* 53: 308-28.

Pizer, Donald. *Realism and Naturalism in Nineteenth-Century American Literature*. Carbondale: Southern Illinois University Press, 1966.

Pound, Louise. "The Dialect of Cooper's Leather-Stocking." *American Speech* 2 (September, 1927): 479-88.

"Questionable Shapes." *Literary World*, 34 (July 1903): 168.

Sears, Donald A. *John Neal*. Boston: Twayne Publishers, 1978.

Sewell, David R. *Mark Twain's Languages: Discourse, Dialogue, and Linguistic Variety*. Berkeley: University of California Press, 1987.

Slotkin, Alan R. *A Study of the Use of Dialect and Diction in Selected Works of Stephen Crane: The Language of New York City and Its Rural Environs*. Unpublished.

Smith, Herbert F., ed. *Literary Criticism of James Russell Lowell*. Lincoln: University of Nebraska Press, 1969.

Spiller, Robert. "Cooper's Notes on Language." *American Speech*, 4: 294-300.

"Stephen Crane Says: Edwin Markham is His First Choice for the American Academy." *New York Journal* (March 31, 1900): 8.

"A Strong Novel by Mr Howells." *Literary Digest*, 29 (November 26, 1904): 729-730.

Thomas, Edith M. "Mr. Howells's Way of Saying Things." *Putnam's Monthly* 4 (July 1908): 443-47.

Trent, William Peterfield et al, ed. "Dialect Writers" in *The Cambridge History of American Literature*. Volume II. New York: Macmillan Co., 1918. Pp. 347-66.

Vanderbilt, Kermit. *The Achievement of William Dean Howells: A Reinterpretation*. Princeton, NJ: Princeton University Press, 1968.

-----------------. "The Conscious Realism of Howells' April Hopes." *American Literary Realism* 3: 53-66.

-----------------. "Howells Studies: Past, or Passing, or to Come." *American Literary Realism* 7: 143-53.

Woodress, James L. *Howells & Italy*. New York: Greenwood Press, 1952.

INDEX

Most references cited within this index are for persons whom Howells knew, critiqued, read, and/or corresponded with. Many sub-references are for the works of those individuals who were writers. The sheer volume of citations to people testifies to the breadth of Howells's knowledge and criticism of past and contemporary literature, as well as the breadth and variety of his reading.

ABOUT THE AUTHOR

Greg Stratman is a writer, the father of three, and a faculty member for the University of Missouri-Rolla and Drury University. His professional experience includes coordinating an ESL program, developing pedagogical manuals, and teaching courses in linguistics, literature, creative writing, professional writing, and ESL verbal skills.

Stratman has published poetry, articles on the English language, course manuals, and over 100 newspaper columns. His current projects include a book-compilation of those columns (written from 1994-1996), a screenplay adaptation of Thomas Hardy's *The Mayor of Casterbridge*, a book on the thinning of the line between right and wrong in America, and a series of ESP booklets on the vocabulary of various disciplinary fields.